Sleep
and
Your Child's
Temperament

Sleep and Your Child's Temperament

Working with your child's personality to achieve blissful sleep

by

Rebecca Michi

Introducing
The Michi Method

Sleep and Your Child's Temperament
Using your child's personality to achieve blissful sleep

Copyright © 2013, by Rebecca Michi
ISBN 978-0-9895079-0-5

Publisher: Rebecca Michi – Children's Sleep Consultant
1718 NW 56th St,
Suite, 208, Seattle, WA, 98107
206-446-7572

ISBN: 978-0-9895079-0-5

Editor: Joan Batty
Jacket Design: www.migzworks.com

Suggestions made in this book are presented as general information and in no
way constitute advice for particular situations and challenges.

Printed in the United States of America

10 9 8 7 6 5 4 3 2

For more information visit: www.rebeccamichi.com

Contents

Finally get some sleep!

Introduction
What You Need To Know About Sleep

This is a book about sleep. Specifically, it's a book about helping babies and small children – and their parents – sleep better, longer, and more reliably. So it makes sense to first wonder why sleep is important and why it sometimes seems so hard to come by.

All creatures sleep. But a giraffe needs fewer than two hours of sleep in every 24 and a sheep needs only 3.8 hours. Cats, on the other hand, sleep half the day away, at 12.1 hours of sleep – though many cats I've known seem to sneak in a few hours more. You, an adult human, need 7 to 8 hours of sleep, according to the National Sleep Foundation. Did you get that much last night?

The 7 to 8 hour figure is adults' average *basal sleep need*. It's what you need day in and day out to be at your best. But you can also accumulate *sleep debt*. That's the zombie-like result of too-little sleep at night and then trying your best to get through the day without nodding off. There is some evidence that sleep debt can be made up at least somewhat by sleeping-in on the weekends. But, of course, as the parent of a small child, your opportunities to sleep-in are few and far between.

Nodding off is a real possibility. Sleep deprivation has been linked to:
- Memory lapses and memory loss
- Depression

- Hallucinations
- Increased blood pressure
- Increased stress hormone levels
- Irritability
- Obesity
- Hand tremors and
- Increased risk of diabetes, fibromyalgia, heart disease and a whole host of other stuff.

If you drive sleep-deprived you are at real risk of having a serious accident and your reaction times are the same as if you were driving drunk! Even if you're not driving, your reaction times, your ability to respond to emergencies, and your overall resilience to the ups and downs of the day are severely impaired. Your body wants to sleep.

Why? Why is sleep so necessary?

Scientists used to think that sleep is needed for bodily repair and rejuvenation and that nothing much goes on during sleep. We know now that's not true. In fact, your brain is as active during some sleep stages as it is when you're awake and thinking hard. That's because during sleep the brain is working at full speed, solidifying what was learned during the day, laying down new memories, and making new synaptic connections as a result of life experiences.

The time when this happens most is during REM sleep. Not all sleep is the same and REM, or Rapid Eye Movement, sleep is when the brain takes over and gets things done. REM sleep is the same as dreaming sleep. It begins about 90 minutes into a night's slumber and repeats every 90 minutes or so throughout the night. In the ideal 8-hour night of sleep, 25% of the time is spent in REM sleep. Your brain needs this time to organize what you've figured out during the day. When you don't get enough sleep, you make yourself less smart than you would like yourself to be.

Goodness knows, there's scarcely another time in life when a person needs to be managing things as well as when a new baby is added to the household or when the trials of toddlerhood are in full swing. But these are just the times when sleep is the hardest to get. What can you do to get back to feeling your best?

The secret, quite reasonably, lies in getting your children to sleep well. As you've undoubtedly discovered, this is not so easy as it seems.

How Much Sleep Do Children Need?

Children need sleep as much as adults do and for the same reason: brain development. The REM sleep that signals high levels of brain activity in adults is even more extensive in babies and toddlers, occupying up to 80% of a newborn's sleep time.

And this sleep time itself is extensive too. Babies 1 to 2 months old need 10 ½ to 18 hours of sleep in every 24. Babies aged 3 months to one year need 9 or 12 hours at night and an additional 2 or 3 hours of sleep in the form of naps during the day. Toddlers from 12

3

months to 3 years old need 12 to 14 hours of sleep per 24 hours, including at least one nap. And preschoolers aged 3 to 5 need 11 to 13 hours of sleep in a day, often all at night. Even elementary-school kids still need 10 to 11 hours of sleep.

Sleep deprivation in children has bad effects, just as it does for grown-ups. It has been linked to stunted growth and attention disorders like ADD and ADHD. Recent studies show that a child who gets insufficient sleep has a higher chance of being obese as a teen and later as an adult.

And then there are the behavior problems associated with overtiredness and sleep deprivation. Here's a sampling:

- Increased temper tantrums
- A greater than usual number of accidents
- Trouble winding down, so that the child becomes more active as the night goes on
- Moodiness, including dramatic highs and lows
- Difficulty concentrating
- Hyperactivity and low impulse control
- Defiance and daredevil risk-taking

(These are behavior problems *in children*, though when adults are overtired they sometimes act like children, too!)

So it makes sense to start as soon as reasonable to teach your child how to fall asleep, how to get back to sleep when awakened, and how to sleep all through the night. People who do not learn healthy sleep habits as children are more likely to struggle with sleep issues as an adult.

Teaching your child to sleep is important. If your child is over nine months old and is still having trouble falling asleep on her own or is waking and needing your attention many times a night, then you are *both* sleep deprived. By taking the little time it takes to sleep train your child, you are actually setting her up for better health as a child and as an adult and contributing to her brain development at the same time.

And if it's been nine months or longer since *you* slept undisturbed all night long, just imagine how you'll feel after getting eight hours of sleep a night.

About This Book

This book is designed to guide you in teaching your child how to fall asleep on his own, get himself back to sleep when he wakes, and stay in bed until it's time to arise. Sounds almost magical, doesn't it?

This book is based on my experience as a parents' sleep consultant. My clients have taught me a lot, including the fact that no two babies are the same. A one-size-fits-all model for sleep-training cannot work for everyone. If you've tried other books and other methods but haven't had success, it's probably not you. And it's not your child.

What I mean is, it's probably *the wrong method* for *your child*. Your child is perfect, of course, and you are trying as hard as you can. But every child has a different style, a different set of default reactions, a different temperament. If you are going to be successful in guiding your child to sleep, it's important to take into account his individual preferences. If you don't do that, it's likely you and he will continue to struggle.

This temperament was there when your child was born and will be there all her life. It is who she is at the most basic level. You cannot change it – and you don't want to, do you? – but you must work with it, not against it. You and your child can become a well-functioning team if you take some time to figure her out.

Central to the methods outlined in this book are three key points:
- Your child has her own unique temperamental profile, which influences everything she does;
- The sleep-training method you use must fit your child's temperament and your own;
- To be effective, any sleep-training method must be used consistently, so don't give up!

There will be bumps in the road. The sleep-training methods described in this book will become your tools for meeting regressions, disruptions, and disturbances as they arise. Just knowing you have a toolbox of techniques will help you to be calmer and less stressed, even in the middle of the night.

How This Book Is Organized

Chapter One is your guide to making the transition from expectant parents to parents of a newborn. You know how hard it was to sleep in the last trimester and how much you looked forward to getting a good night's sleep. Now that the baby is born, it looks like the sleepless nights will continue a bit longer. In Chapter One, I give you some advice for managing those first few weeks.

Chapter Two introduces temperament. It talks about the different styles typical of most children, how these affect sleep and sleep-training, and how to decide which temperament is your child's.

In Chapter Three discusses routines, which will help your child fall asleep more readily. Chapter Four considers where to put your baby to bed, including the pros and cons of co-sleeping.

In Chapter Five, we'll examine sleep-training methods you may have heard about or even tried and I'll share The Michi Method, designed especially to fit your child's temperament and your family's situation.

In Chapter Six we'll tackle sleep issues in toddlers and in Chapter Seven, sleep issues in preschoolers.

Chapter Eight is devoted to sleep disturbances, like nightmares, sleepwalking and night terrors. Chapter Ten takes on naps.

In Chapter Ten we consider problems with waking up, including waking too early and waking up unhappy.

And in Chapter Eleven, we consider all the other things that can disrupt a good night's sleep for you and your child, including vacation travel, the birth of a new sibling, and other events.

As a mother myself and as a sleep consultant in private practice, I've seen how difficult getting children to sleep can be and how it can affect not only your evenings but your daytimes, your work life and your relationships within the family. I want the best for you. And I know the best starts with a good night's sleep.

Let's begin!

Chapter One
Bringing Baby Home

Few events are more exciting and more terrifying than bringing home a new baby. Both parents are exhausted and both parents need sleep. Their infant, on the other hand, doesn't seem to understand.

Let's sort out what you need to know about infants' sleep when you bring a new baby home.

Newborn Sleep

According to the children's hospital at Stanford University, newborns sleep about 16 hours in every 24, about evenly divided between daytime hours and nighttime. The thing is, infants have no concept of "day" and "night" and are likely to be awake and engaging at any time.

Add to this the fact that infants' stomachs are small and their need for nourishment is great. They must feed every three or four hours around the clock for the first three months or so, or until they weigh about 12 pounds. Only then can babies start to stretch nighttime sleeping into something that approximates "through the night

Sleeping Through The Night
Sleeping through the night is the Holy Grail of parenthood. Probably you were asked by some idiot

in your baby's first week, "Is he sleeping through the night yet?"

Although everyone realizes that getting a baby to sleep through the night is some sort of milestone, not everyone agrees on what "sleeping through the night" is. I recently asked on my Facebook page and Twitter what parents think defines sleeping through the night. The answers varied from "eight hours of continuous sleep" to "not getting me up before 5." I know that some families say that as long as their child goes straight back to sleep after a midnight feed and they are not being awakened more than twice, they are sleeping through the night.

Sleep experts say sleeping five hours or more after midnight is classified as "sleeping through the night." Personally I disagree. Most adults need more than five hours a night. I believe sleeping through the night means your child is not getting you up at all between the time you put her down at night until your personal acceptable wake up time in the morning.

It's obvious that sleeping through the night all the way till morning will take longer to achieve than just sleeping for five hours at a stretch. It will depend on your child's weight and temperament more than on anything you do to encourage longer sleep.

Something that parents are sometimes advised to do to get an infant to sleep longer at night is to feed solid foods before bed. Sad to say, this is an old wives' tale without any basis in actual fact. In addition, feeding solids to an infant younger than five or six months old is not a good idea at any time, day or night. Infants need the nutrition of breast milk or formula exclusively - so exclusively that any substitution of solid food results in poorer nutrition. And a small baby's mouth and throat are shaped only for liquid foods up until about five months. Introducing solid foods before the mouth and throat are shaped to accept them can result in choking.

Another practice you want to avoid in your efforts to get an infant to sleep through the night is putting her to bed with a bottle, or just propping a bottle in the crib when she wakes in the night. Doing this can cause choking, ear infections, and decay of those first tiny teeth.

Decide on your own benchmark for "sleeping through the night" and realize that sooner or later you and your child will get there. This is not a race.

Newborns' Sleep Stages
Babies, like adults, have stages of sleep that change throughout a sleep episode (nighttime or day time). Depending on the stage, the baby may be very still or thrash around. As we discussed in Chapter One, there are two types of sleep for everybody: REM or rapid eye movement sleep and non-REM sleep. Babies experience REM and non-REM sleep but in different proportions than adults.

Newborn babies' REM sleep takes up fully half of their sleeping time, or about 8 hours. This is dreaming sleep in adults and children, so we assume that babies also dream during this time. We have no idea, though, what they could possibly dream of!

Just as in adults and children, babies' non-REM sleep has four stages, corresponding to four levels of sleep. In Stage 1, the baby is dozing and his eyes may open and close. In Stage 2, the baby is in light sleep and may move around or startle to sudden sounds. Stage 3 sleep in deeper and the baby is limp and quiet and does not move. Stage 4 is even deeper and still the baby is quiet and unmoving. A baby starts at Stage 1, of course, then moves ever deeper through Stages 2, 3, and 4, then returns to Stage 3, then 2, and then enters REM sleep.

After REM, the baby goes back to Stages 2, then 3, then 4, and so the cycle continues until the child wakes. As babies move up the scale from deeper stages to lighter ones, they may wake up.

Another sleep element is the cycle of melatonin production. Starting at about three months a child's body will start producing melatonin, the hormone which induces sleep. Prior to this age, babies have none of the circadian rhythm associated with a day-night sleep pattern.

Once production of melatonin kicks in at about three months, its presence in the body follows a predictable pattern. It rises in the evening, is highest during the middle of the night and then gradually reduces during the later part of the night and early morning. Melatonin production is another step along the path to sleeping through the night.

Because the body's release of melatonin is triggered by light levels, you can support the action of melatonin by having darkness - or at least dimness - as part of your child's bedtime and naptime routines. In addition, children who are exposed to daylight in the morning and early afternoons have better melatonin production when evening falls, so try to get outdoors every day.

When a newborn wakes up at the end of a sleep cycles, she might enter a quiet alert phase. The baby lies still in her crib, but is awake and is taking in the environment. During this quiet alert time, a baby may look at objects and make small sounds. This phase usually progresses to an active alert phase in which the baby moves more actively. And after this phase is a crying phase. It's best, naturally, to get to your child before she starts to cry.

Crying

There are different types of cry. One of the first tasks new parents face is figuring out what their infant's cries mean. Many parents have a hard time telling which cry is what, so don't feel badly if you can't. Some children are not as easy as others to figure out. So do the best you can here.

The hunger cry starts with a little cough. Maybe two of three of these. And then it is really rhythmical. Cry and pause. Cry and pause.

The pain of cry is long and loud and urgent. It may begin suddenly, stop for a little, and start again. You sense that something is wrong, and it is!

The mantra cry is a repetitive waa, waa, waa but without the urgency of the pain cry. It's a cry of overtiredness, or boredom, or frustration, or overstimulation.

The Mommy-I-Need-You-Now cry is the loud, urgent cry of a child who needs attention for whatever reason. He's reaching the edge of his ability to manage himself and he needs someone to help him calm down. This cry, the MINYN cry, is your signal to action even when you know your child is not in pain or hungry.

If your newborn is on a crying jag but doesn't seem to be in pain and doesn't seem hungry, what can you do? Try soothing him with a warm bath or a massage. Undressing your child can sometimes change his mood, as can stepping outdoors or moving into another room. Rocking is a time-honored way to soothe an infant. You might find that rocking backwards and forwards works better than rocking side-to-side - or vice versa! Consider changing your child's diaper, offering a pacifier, bouncing on an exercise ball, going for a stroller ride (even in the house), offering a feed, swaddling your baby or singing.

Do what you can to cheer your little person. I don't advise you leaving a newborn to cry for any length of time. Having said that, sometimes you may need to step away and have a breather. An infant's cry can become too much to listen to if it's for long periods of time. If that's the case, make sure your child is safe in his crib or bassinet and step away for a few minutes. You'll be far more effective at dealing with the crying after having a quick breather than you would have had you stayed.

Never Missing A Cry…

A baby monitor is so often on the list of must haves for new parents. But do you really need one?

Look at the layout of your home. Babies cry *loudly*. Is there anywhere in your house where you won't be able to hear your child when he cries? If you can hear your baby in the places you're likely to be when your little one is sleeping, then you don't really need a monitor.

Not only that, but even babies who are not crying are still noisy. They grunt, moan, squirm, burp and fart, all whilst asleep. And you don't need to be alerted to all this. You don't need to jump at every noise your child makes. If you have a monitor in your bedroom and your child has one in her room you may as well be sleeping next to her. You will hear every noise she makes. Chances are that this will wake you for no reason. You may spend quite a bit of your night awake listening to your little one noisily sleeping.

Of course, new parents are nervous. It's easy to think that every sound is significant. But really, you don't want to jump out of bed as soon as you hear your little one make a noise. Always wait for that really urgent Mommy-I-Need-You-Now cry. And unless you live in a 30-room mansion, you can hear *that* without a monitor.

You might have got a monitor as a gift, and so the cost of buying one isn't an issue in your decision to use a monitor or not. But there's another really good reason to avoid using even a gift monitor. Monitors use DECT technology - that stands for "Digital Enhanced Cordless Telecommunications" electromagnetic energy. This isn't something you want to expose your children to too much of. While the science is not clear, the effect of excess electromagnetic energy has been questioned for a long time. If you would hesitate to live right under high voltage power lines, then you should also hesitate to use a baby monitor.

In addition, baby monitors pose a strangulation hazard, since most include some sort of cord that dangles within the crib.

If you're going to use a monitor you want to make sure that it's as far away from the crib as possible. I would also make sure that you don't have any other electrical appliances in the child's room, like a computer, television, or HEPA filter.

Don't think that you must have a monitor because "everyone else" has one. I know many families who have never used one. I didn't use one when my daughters were little. We didn't really have the need, even with one of our daughters sleeping on another floor from us.

If you cannot hear your child or if your child has a medical condition that requires constant vigilance, then monitors can give you peace of mind. But pay attention to those hazards even then.

Getting A Newborn To Sleep

As a children sleep specialist, newborn sleep is something I am asked about many times and though I help people sleep train their children up to six years old, I don't advise sleep training a newborn. The first three months really are the fourth trimester and I advise you to do whatever you can to get as much sleep as you can without worrying about your baby's sleep schedule.

Having said that, there is quite a bit you can do to encourage positive sleep habits. I'm going to outline for you my favorite sleep tips for newborns. These will give you confidence that you are doing all you can to get as much sleep as you can. Also you'll be setting up some great sleep associations for your infant that will pay off when it *is* time for sleep training.

Okay, let's get started.

Begin With The Room

Set up a great sleep environment. Keep the sleeping environment between 65 and 70°- this is definitely warm enough for your infant. You don't want him becoming too hot or too cold.

Dear Rebecca -
I have a daughter who is almost 4 months old. She consistently has been sleeping through the night. However over the past few weeks she's been waking repeatedly to eat. She is genuinely hungry when she wakes.

Do you have any recommendations on how to get her back on her routine? Is it time to start some rice cereal?

Dear Mum -
I'd look at her daytime feeds. You want to try and stretch the feeds out to between every three and four hours. Stretch the time out between feeds during the day and avoid snacking. A child who snacks during the day will snack during the night.

Studies show that children do not sleep any longer when rice cereal is introduced. Rice cereal is very easily digested and doesn't hang around in the stomach.

Good luck! I'm sure this problem will go away soon.

One way to see if your infant is too cold or hot is to feel his chest. Often little hands or head feel very cool, so check his chest to get a real idea if your baby is hot or cold.

Swaddle Your Baby

Infants are born with the startle reflex, as a reaction to noises or movement, especially the laying down movement of putting them to bed. They fling their arms out as if they were stopping themselves from falling.

And as babies go through the different stages of the sleep cycle they can startle too, and wake themselves up. One way to control the startle reflex is to wrap the infant snugly so his arms are held in place at his side. This is called "swaddling."

Swaddling can also be very calming and relaxing for your infant. She has spent nine months snuggled up inside Mother and suddenly having arms and legs which freely move can be scary. Remember your infant doesn't have any control over her limbs. When her arms fly out in the startle reflex she really doesn't know what's going on with her own body. So swaddling is not only good at nighttime, it's also a great way to calm a crying baby.

Here's how to do it. Spread out a thin receiving blanket and place the baby with his head in one corner. Some parents fold this corner down to make a straight edge behind the baby's shoulders. Fold the bottom corner up to cover his feet and legs, then fold the blanket's left corner over the baby's right arm and side and tuck it snugly under his body on his left side (your right). Pull the remaining corner across his body, making his left arm lie snugly along his left side, and tuck the free end under his body. The baby now looks something like a burrito with a head sticking out. Since you will lay your child down to sleep on his back, the entire package should hold together pretty well.

Go With The Flow

If you're trying to get your infant into her own sleep space, either a bassinet or crib, but you find that she would rather be held, then just hold her as much as you can. Try wearing your infant in a carrier. You're not spoiling your baby to keep her near you in the first few weeks of life.

Sometimes you need to get yourself something to eat or you need to jump in the shower, though. You can help your baby accept being put down by putting her down on a crib sheet that smells like you. Wear the crib sheet under your shirt for an hour or two or even place it under the covers of your bed for a night. Then, when you use this sheet in your child's crib or bassinet, it will smell of you. The sense of smell is very important to babies so this technique can actually have a good effect.

Don't worry too much if you find yourself nursing or feeding your infant to sleep. He's so young it's fine to do. Don't think that is the only way you get him to sleep though. Every day try putting him down to sleep drowsy but awake. You never know... he may be able to get himself to sleep.

But if he can't fall asleep on his own, don't worry! Just pick him up and maybe rock him to sleep. Did you know that rocking side to side (in a swaying motion) is more relaxing than rocking back to front (as you would in a rocking chair)? When your baby has finally fallen asleep pop him back into the crib. Keep your hands on him for a little while just in case you need to pick him up or give him a little reassuring rub.

It takes 20 minutes for an infant to fall into a deep sleep. If you rush off as soon as you put your infant into the crib and you keep having to go back to help her get back to sleep, this becomes very frustrating for both of you. Instead of hurrying away, just wait in her room until she is in a deep sleep. Your baby will fall into a deep sleep quicker if you are there to help her at the moment she needs it and it is less frustrating for you.

Don't worry about setting up bad sleep habits and associations with your infant. You really must do whatever you need to do to get as much sleep as you can get.

Back To Sleep
Always, always, always put your infant down to sleep on his back with his feet towards the bottom of the crib. Tuck in a bedding tightly and do not use blankets, bumpers or pillows. All of this reduces the risk of SIDS.

Dear Rebecca –
My one week old makes gurgling noises and starts to cry every time we lay her on her back to sleep. This is after we get a few good burps and she rarely spits up so I don't think it's reflux. She sleeps fine upright on our shoulder or in a car seat, swing or bouncy seat.

Her older sister was the same way and she only ever slept on her tummy on our chests. I would like this baby to learn to sleep on her back in a bassinet and eventually in a crib.

Any tips or ideas? Is this normal for all newborns?

Dear Mum -
It sounds like silent reflux to me. Reflux doesn't have to have spitting up. Often the flap, which holds the stomach contents in the stomach, is not well developed in newborns and they are often uncomfortable. Talk with your doctor.

But I would suggest letting her sleep in the swing and in a carrier. You may want to have a look at using a foam wedge; do you have a friend you could borrow one from? Sleeping on an incline may be helpful to infants or uncomfortable due to reflux. Good luck!

Sleep When Your Infant Sleeps

This really is so important. Your newborn may sleep for up to 16 hours a day but not for very long at any one time. He will wake many, many times - maybe as often as every hour! This means you'll only be able to sleep for short periods of time. Expect this. Don't fight it or let it stress you out.

Try having a "babymoon" - like a honeymoon but with your newborn. Plan to spend a few days or even a few weeks in bed all day with your infant. Devote this time to establishing feeding and getting some much-needed sleep. If you can get someone to be around to take care of things and bring you lunches and snacks while you're on your babymoon, so much the better!

Don't feel that you owe it to people to let them in any time of the day or evening to see you and the baby. Set some limits. Of course, your friends will want to stop by but let them know times when it's fine for them to visit and don't let them in at other times. Some parents put a note on the front door letting people know that they are trying to sleep.

And remember, if your mother or mother-in-law is there to help out, make certain she helps out with *your* needs. That might include "helping with the baby" but it might mean doing the dishes and walking the dog. Your big job right now is to get what sleep you can and to bond with your child.

If you have an older child or for some other reason are unable to take a babymoon, make the most of friends and family who want to help you out. This is not the time to say, "Oh no, I'm okay, thanks!" This is the time to say, "Yes, please, I need all the help I can get!"

Possible Problems

Understand that even if you do everything right (and, really, who of us does?), problems will still arise. Here is a quick review of problems with newborns you might be concerned about.

Infant Reflux

Reflux is heartburn. Have you ever had heartburn? Nasty isn't it? Can you imagine having only just been brought into this world and having virtually constant heartburn? No wonder infants with reflux have that shrill cry.

Reflux is caused when the muscles, which connect the stomach and esophagus, or immature, allowing the stomach's contents to reenter the esophagus. As the stomach contains mainly acid, it burns.

It's estimated that up to 60% of newborns suffer reflux in the first weeks of life. It makes those first weeks hard - no, tough - no, *almost unbearable!* An infant with reflux cries - a lot! - and the sound of that cry is also very different, more shrill and piercing than an ordinary cry. It seems to go right through you.

A baby with reflux may experience frequent spitting up (even vomiting), sour breath, fussiness and crying sometimes, poor feeding habits, very small feeds, and a preference for being held upright - and, of course, the painful cries. An infant with reflux may have excessively poor sleep habits both during the day and night.

What can you do to help? Reflux will eventually go away. But in the meantime, there are tricks you can do to help your baby feel better.

- Small frequent feedings are certainly the way to go. You don't want the stomach becoming too full.

- Feed your child with them sat at around a 30° angle, not lying down flat.

- If you're nursing and you have an overactive letdown - which can really bother an infant with reflux - try nipple shields when nursing. It may slow things down for your child making feed times more comfortable.

- Hold your child upright after you have fed him. Give that milk a chance to stay in his tummy.

- A sleeping wedge can be one of the most important pieces of equipment you can get. These permit a child to sleep at an incline, making her more comfortable and less likely to spit up. The wedge might make sleep actually possible. These wedges are available through your pediatrician or hospital.

- One mom found baby yoga to be incredibly helpful. Sometimes you need to think away from conventional remedies and think outside the box.

- Try putting a cummerbund around your infant's tummy. The pressure against the tummy can make your child really comfortable. Just make sure this isn't too tight. You can get a smaller effect by wearing your infant in a carrier or sling.

Remember to talk to your pediatrician about your baby's troubles. There is medication available that can help and if your child is in a lot of pain, you certainly want to relieve that. Don't think of medication as a last resort. There are many children who respond well to medication.

And most of all, remember that this is something which will get better. It doesn't last forever.

Colic

The symptoms of colic are very similar to those of infant reflux, in fact, colic and reflux may be the same thing. Not much clear is known about colic. It might be that in colic the problem is gas, not spitting up. Like the infant with reflux, the colicky baby cries inconsolably, especially in the afternoon or evening.

Like reflux, colic appears most often in the first weeks of life and disappears as children grow past about six months. Episodes of colic (and also reflux) can be triggered by what a nursing mother eats, so be careful about eating garlic, onions, broccoli, peppers and spicy foods.

Just as with reflux, talk with your pediatrician about medications, including over the counter medicines, that can help with colic.

Sudden Infant Death Syndrome
Sudden Infant Death Syndrome (SIDS) or "crib death" is the death of a seemingly healthy baby without any warning. SIDS is every parent's nightmare.

Most babies who die of SIDS are under six months of age. The riskiest age for SIDS is between 2 and 4 months. Danger of SIDS declines to nearly zero at one year.

Because SIDS is so unexpected, its causes have been a mystery. Several factors are associated with SIDS, however: low birth weight, including prematurity, a recent cold or other respiratory problem, and undetected brain anomalies. In addition, babies of African American or Native American descent have a higher risk of SIDS. Research continues to identify more risk factors.

Obviously, you can't do much about the risk factors that have been identified so far. But there are things you can do to lower the possibility of SIDS. Some of these things may be possible in your situation and some might not. So just do the best you can and what you're comfortable with.

- Consider having the child sleep in the same room as the adults for the first six months, so you are more aware of baby's breathing.

- Consider using a pacifier if your child will accept one. Pacifier use has been found to reduce the risk of SIDS.

- Use a firm crib mattress that is safety approved.

- Keep soft objects, toys, and loose bedding out of the crib. This means no pillows, quilts, sheepskins, or bumpers.

- If you must use a blanket, place your baby at the foot of the crib with the blanket no higher than the baby's chest and the blanket tucked under the crib mattress to keep it in place. (Better yet, don't use the blanket but dress baby in a blanket sleeper.)

- Don't smoke around the baby or permit others to do so.

- Avoid overheating the room during sleep or dressing babies too warmly. Keep babies on the cool side.

- ALWAYS lay your child down to sleep on his back at least until he's a year old. Don't worry, though, about repositioning your child through the night if your child can roll over and does.

Avoid products that claim to reduce the risk of SIDS. These are not tested and just prey on parents' fears.

According to the Centers for Disease Control, since 1990 the incidence of SIDS deaths in the U.S. has fallen by 50%. Currently about 2,250 babies die of

SIDS in the United States every year. This sounds like a big number but the CDC also reports 4 million babies are born each year in the U.S. So the incidence of SIDS is only about 6 in 10,000. This is pretty small. Odds are, your baby will celebrate her first birthday and all will be well.

Of course, even one SIDS death is too many. The steps you can take to lower your child's risk are simple to follow so try to do that.

Quick Tips For Newborn Sleep

Tag Team
It may take a while to get your child down to sleep for the first few nights. Anything under an hour is classed as normal.

Tag teaming will help. Have your partner come in to take over after a set amount of time - 20 minutes is good. You'll have 20 minutes to relax and decompress before you go back in for another 20 minutes. Make sure the takeover is quiet and calm, with no talking with your partner. One comes in and the other leaves straightaway.

Use Ear Plugs
Yes, your child is going to cry. And crying is designed by Mother Nature to bother you. So wear ear plugs. You will still be able to hear your child, but the ear

Dear Rebecca -
Our baby is almost 3 months old. She's been having meltdowns in the past week prior to each nap and bedtime. She gets tired quickly in just one hour and needs a nap. She takes four naps a day.

She goes from a happy baby straight into a crying and miserable baby area and no tired signs. I assume this is developmental?

Anyhow, we had to swaddle her to calm her down although we did not swaddle her since she was two weeks old. She sleeps so much better now when swaddle.

Should we continue to swaddle her even at this age?

Dear Dad -
Some children show tired signs, others don't. Some show them 20 minutes before they need to sleep. Others show signs only as they are becoming overtired. If your child isn't showing you any tired signs watch the clock and make sure you have started your nap routine before she becomes overtired.

I would certainly continue with the swaddle for sleep times. You just want to make sure that you are no longer swaddling when she is able to roll over.

plugs will take the edge off the crying whilst you are in the room with them.

A calm, less-stressed parent is a more effective parent. Use the tools at your disposal!

Avoid Overtiredness

An overtired infant can really struggle to fall asleep and remain asleep. Initially, it may help you to watch the clock and get your infant down for a nap every hour-and-a-half, following a pretty rigid schedule.

Don't worry, though, because it won't always be like this. As your child grows she will start to show you tired signs. You'll be able to see when your child is tired by simply observing her fussiness, rubbing her eyes, staring off into space, and so on.

Never Wake A Sleeping Baby?

This all depends. If your child is gaining weight at a steady pace and by two months of age has regained the initial post-birth weight loss, then I wouldn't advise waking your child if he's sleeping longer than usual. Do wake your child at the five-hour mark, however. He does need to feed!

However, if your child is spending lots of time during the night awake, then he may need to sleep less during the day. Infants don't have a good sense of day and night and your baby may have his schedule backwards.

Also, if your child has not gained the weight he should, then you don't want him to miss or delay a feed. Remember that with his tiny tummy he can't eat more to make up for missed feeds. Talk to your pediatrician if you're concerned about weight gain.

Keep A Sleep Diary

If you're not sleeping well, your memory will not be at its best. And if you and your child are both struggling to sleep your frustration level will be high. You might lose track of the happy moments and you might think only of the bad times.

So keep a sleep diary. When you keep track of when your child sleeps and when she wakes, you will start to see patterns. You will start to understand what sets her off and what seems to calm her down.

The example diary on the next page is one way to format this, but you can also keep a more conventional, essay-style diary or keep notes in a calendar program. You can also find sleep diary apps for iPhone and such. Look around and find something that fits your needs.

Your newborn sleep diary will make fun reading later, when your baby is finally sleeping through the night and things have settled down a bit.

Infants grow quickly and soon the challenges you're having today will be replaced by new and different ones. You will start to detect a pattern in these challenges, a pattern that points to your child's basic temperament.

Temperament is such a key issue in sleep that we'll look at that next.

There's a downloadable sleep diary form on my website at www.rebeccamichi.com

SAMPLE BABY'S SLEEP DIARY

Date: _____

Hours awake for the day: _____

Hours asleep for the day: _____

Time asleep	Comments

Time awake	Comments

Time asleep	Comments

Time awake	Comments

Chapter Two
Your Child's Temperament

Your little person is like no one else. She's special in so many ways and she was special right from Day One.

So it makes sense that a One-Size-Fits-All plan of sleep training probably won't work. In fact, if some sort of cookie-cutter plan did work, it would be just luck. But you need more than luck. You need results. And to get the best results, start first with your child. Who is she? What's she like?

Nine Basic Traits

Sixty years ago, Stella Chess and Alexander Thomas launched the New York Longitudinal Study to investigate the beginnings of personality. They discovered that people display nine traits. These traits seem to be present at birth and to be stable over one's entire life. These traits form a person's default position, his "presets."

A person could display these traits across a range from low to high. The traits are neither good nor bad, since low and high aspects of each of these can be useful or a hurdle in different situations. The nine traits are these:

- **Activity:** A person might be constantly on the move or more relaxed, even lethargic.

- **Rhythmicity:** A person might easily fall into dependable patterns of eating, sleeping and elimination or might display more random and unpredictable patterns.
- **Approach/withdrawal:** A person might be eager for new experiences or very reluctant and reserved.
- **Adaptability:** A person might handle change easily or might react badly to any change in plans.
- **Intensity:** A person might react dramatically to life situations or might be more unruffled.
- **Mood:** A person might be usually negative in outlook or usually positive. She might be mercurial, shifting moods rapidly, or more steady.
- **Persistence and attention span:** A person might give up quickly or stick with a task doggedly. He may be very focused or may flit from one idea to another.
- **Distractibility:** A person might be easily distracted by outside interruptions or so focused it's hard to shake her out of her thoughts.
- **Sensory threshold:** A person might be sensitive to things like noises, lights, or textures or might be less aware and less bothered by such things.

So think for a moment about your child. Even newborns show evidence of most of these traits, though some of these might be harder to detect in a very young baby. These are your child's inborn traits that shape how she reacts to everyday events, including how easily she falls asleep.

Think also about yourself and your child's other parent. Because the nine traits are part of a person's basic make-up, they are there throughout life. You or your partner might react differently to your child's behavior, not because of the child but because of your own innate responses to things. Your child's crying might set one of your off more than the other. One or the other of you might have a shorter fuse, might be more easily frustrated, or might be more disturbed by a small child's constant demands, not because of any personality flaws but because that's just who you or your partner are.

Knowing your own presets, your partner's presets, and figuring out your child's presets will give you clues about how to handle situations in ways that will be satisfying to all of you. It will also give you an idea of the best way - for you and for your child - to manage sleep training.

When Traits Conflict

These nine traits are preset *and* they are inherited. Personality profiles tend to run in families. Your child may have the same traits or many of the same traits as you or as his other parent. This can raise some interesting conflicts.

If both you and your child, for example, are naturally intense and dramatic your home could quickly become theatrical, as each of you demands attention and feels deeply the importance of your points of view. If both you and your child are strongly regular in your habits but also inflexible, there may be problems if one of you is hungry or sleepy at times the other is not.

At the same time, of course, your child's trait pattern might be more like the trait pattern of his other parent. You might be the odd one out. It can feel like you're being ganged up on - or being left out - if your child and your spouse seem to be on the same wavelength but both on a different wavelength than you.

Just knowing that these nine traits exist and knowing your child's trait pattern may seem similar to your own or to the trait pattern of your partner helps to understand some of the glitches that occur in your family relationships. Realizing that these are preset and permanent helps us accept the people we love as they are. We cannot change them, though we can change how we react to them and we can help our children learn more adaptive ways of responding.

Temperament

Chess and Thomas noticed that the nine traits tend to cluster into three distinct groupings called temperaments. These groupings are stable across cultures and seem as valid today as when they were identified in the 1950s. Nearly two-thirds of all children (and adults too) fit into one of the three temperaments, with the other third matching a combination of temperaments.

The three temperaments are Easy, Difficult, and Slow-To-Warm-Up.

The Easy Child

Forty percent of children are "easy" or "flexible." On the nine traits, the Easy Child tends to have a pattern similar to this:

Activity: Medium level of activity maybe even placid

Rhythmicity: Reliable patterns of eating, sleeping, waking and elimination

Approach/withdrawal: Very open to new experiences

Adaptability: Very adaptable; not bothered by change

Intensity: Little drama

Mood: Generally sunny mood

Persistence and attention span: Attentive and willing to try

Distractibility: Moderate levels of focus: neither easily distracted nor unshakably focused

Sensory threshold: Not bothered by things very much

The Easy Child can go everywhere without much fuss. This is the baby who sleeps in a corner while his parents attend a party. This is the toddler who racks up frequent flyer miles, just because he's such a pleasant little guy to take everywhere. This child eats without difficulty or pickiness, gets along well with

Dear Rebecca –
Our son is 16 months old. He has always been a challenge. The least sound wakes him, he cries a lot, and if he gets just a little bit overtired he's up for hours. Frankly, we're sick of this. We'd like to have another child but we can't imagine going through this again – or having two sleepless kids at the same time. Will he outgrow this? What are the chances another baby would act differently?

Dear Mum –
Naturally you're frustrated. And it might be that your little guy will always be a bit of a challenge: he may be temperamentally "difficult" and more demanding and opinionated than other children. As he grows, you can help him manage his feelings better and show him ways to be more relaxed.

Since temperament is inherited, it's possible that a second child will be challenging too. But it's more likely that your second child will be easier to get along with. Researchers call this "regression to the mean." Probably the next baby will be much less of a challenge.

Best wishes!

others, and enjoys doing new things. As this child grows up, he adapts quickly to childcare or preschool.

No temperament is perfect, however. The Easy Child might not ever get quite what she wants because she's so accommodating. She may not tell you when something's bothering her because she's so used to just going along. As your Easy Child grows up, you may need to push her a little bit to help her achieve her potential and win a little stardom.

This child may sleep train fairly easily and may adapt to new sleeping situations without drama.

The Difficult Child

Chess and Thomas estimate that 10 percent of children are "difficult" or "spirited." On the nine traits, the Difficult Child tends to have a pattern similar to this:

Activity: High to moderate activity, often restless and impulsive

Rhythmicity: A pattern of no pattern - demands food, sleeps and wakes at all hours and elimination is unpredictable

Approach/withdrawal: Reactive around new people and situations

Adaptability: Unhappy with change; changes may set the child off

Intensity: Very intense reactions; a regular drama queen

Mood: Often negative, though sunny moods are brilliantly happy

Persistence and attention span: Easily frustrated

Distractibility: Intensely focused or easily distracted; has difficulty going with the flow

Sensory threshold: Often bothered by clothing tags, noises, scary things.

The Difficult Child is high-strung and demanding. As a baby, she cries quite a bit for what seems like no reason. It is difficult to take this child out and about, since she may poop or need a feeding at unexpected times. The Difficult toddler may struggle to control her impulses and may run out in the street, bite, or stage a meltdown without much warning. The Difficult Child may seem sensitive to particular foods or eat from a limited menu.

The Difficult Child is a handful and he requires careful parenting to help him moderate his demands and learn strategies to get along with others. But he also tends to be creative and interesting, with lots of energy. He's a child who knows what he wants out of life and is determined to get it. You can't fault him for that!

This child may pose a challenge for sleep training and he may continue to have sleep issues throughout childhood.

The Slow-To-Warm-Up Child
About 15 percent of children are "slow-to-warm-up" or "reserved." On the nine traits, the Slow-To-

Warm-Up Child tends to have a pattern similar to this:

Activity: Moderate to low activity, often inactive in a way that seems disinterested

Rhythmicity: Generally regular in sleeping, eating and elimination

Approach/withdrawal: Shy and uncomfortable around new people and unhappy in new situations

Adaptability: Unhappy with change; changes may be met by "turtling" into a shell

Intensity: Fussy, clingy behavior can reach an intense level but can also seem oblivious and "not present"

Mood: Often negative in public, though happy enough in familiar surroundings

Persistence and attention span: Often very detail-oriented and absorbed

Distractibility: Strongly dislikes interruption

Sensory threshold: Often bothered by intrusive sensations and imagined threats

The Slow-To-Warm-Up Child is careful about everything. As a baby, she may seem like an Easy Child, since she is quiet much of the time. But a trip to the market or a visit from Grandma may be a Big Deal for this child and may completely throw her into a tizzy. The Slow-to-Warm-Up Child may have

Dear Rebecca –
We have twins. They are 10 months old.
Anders is easy-going and cheerful. He sleeps
well, eats well, and pretty much goes with the
flow. Sven is calm and happy too, except if we
have a babysitter. Then he completely melts
down. If we go out in the evening we can
pretty much count on Sven being awake and
bawling when we get home. I'm going back to
work full-time soon and the boys will be in
daycare. Right now can't see how Sven will
manage. He might cry the entire time and
never take a nap. Help!

Dear Mum and Dad –
This sounds like separation anxiety to me. This
kicks in at about 10 months, so Sven is right
on schedule. You may see the same thing
soon in his brother too.

If you can delay going back to work for
another six months, your boys will work
through their anxiety in their familiar
environment. If you can't delay, then they will
adapt. No long term harm will result, so long
as you continue to give the boys plenty of
support and attention (but not smothering!)
when you're home.

"Easy" children like your twins adapt pretty
quickly to changes even during times when
separation anxiety is strongest. Good luck!

difficulty playing with others, preferring to stick close to his parents. This child may need to sit on the sidelines of any new activity before venturing to participate. The Slow-To-Warm-Up Child may want to wear only familiar clothing and only eat familiar foods.

The Slow-To-Warm-Up Child is not so much difficult but exasperating. Everything is worth close examination and consideration for this child and tiny changes are enough to derail an entire afternoon. But this also means that this cautious little body is a thinker. He won't rush into trouble or get in over his head. Instead he may be an excellent observer of what's going on and be able to understand others quite well.

This child be difficult to sleep train at first but then settle into a pattern and stick with it. Changes will disrupt this child, though, like changes to his bed or room.

The Other 35 Percent
Your child may not be clearly Easy, or Difficult or Slow-To-Warm-Up. Your child might exhibit a combination of traits that doesn't quickly fall into one temperament or another. That's okay.

The point is to notice. See what tends to drive your child's reactions and responses and his level of upset or calm. These are not casual occurrences - these represent traits that likely will be life-long. The sooner you realize who your child really is and how she tends to react, the better able you'll be to present your parenting in ways she can accept and that you both can be happy with.

Look at the Trait Chooser on the next page and see what your child's presets (and your own presets) might be. Notice that a child's temperament cannot be determined just by selecting a vertical column since the traits. In fact, the Chooser is only intended to help you see your child more clearly, in all his or her variety and delightfulness.

Sleep Training With Temperament In Mind

It comes as no surprise now that children of different temperaments react to sleep training in different ways. Obviously, it will be helpful to you as you work to solve sleep issues that you take into account your child's usual patterns of behavior.

Sleep Training The Easy Child

The Easy Child generally takes to sleep training with little trouble. This is the infant who may sleep through the night at just a few weeks old and the toddler who hums and sings himself to sleep without fuss.

Of course, the Easy Child can lull a parent into complacency. It's still important to pay more attention to sleep details when your easy baby is teething, has been ill, or is sleeping in a new place. But your task at these times is just to move your Easy Child back to her default position. That's not too hard to do.

The Trait Chooser: Your Child's Typical Expression Of Nine Personality Traits

YOUR CHILD'S...	High Expression					Low Expression
Play behavior	Frantic	Always "on"	Busy	Thoughtful	Quiet	Uninterested
Rhythm for feeding, sleeping and elimination	Set-your-watch predictable		Ordinary predictability		Totally unpredictable	
Openness to new people	Go with anyone	Very friendly	Quick to warm up	Cautious	Upset	Terrified
Adaptability to new situations	No-Rules adaptable	Change on a dime	Easily accepts change	Takes a moment to adapt	Rigid	Meltdown
Level of emotional drama	Emotional rollercoaster	Frequent meltdowns	Ordinary highs and lows	Unfazed by most things	Little emotion	Stone faced
Overall happiness	Cheery	Usually cheery	Pretty happy	Frequently unhappy	Crabby	Sad
Level of effort and persistence	Obsessive	Driven	Steady worker	Tries	Gives up quickly	Won't even try
Attention span and focus	Locked in	Reluctant to switch attention	Is in control of focus	Focus control not fully developed	Frequent loss of focus	Scattered
Level of pickiness and rigidity	Issues seem to paralyze action	Issues interfere with daily life	Issues with food, sound, light	Some issues, often with food	A few issues with some things	Anything is fine

Dear Rebecca –
I am a pretty particular person. You might say I'm driven, sort of Type A, and I have very high standards. My partner – who I adore – is so relaxed he sometimes seems nonexistent. Anything is okay for him. He can even sleep on airplanes – something I never can do.

Our daughter is just like my partner. She's two and she falls asleep at the drop of a hat. She always has. We never had to sleep-train her. This might sound great but I'm worried. With school so competitive these days, is her relaxed manner likely to stick with her? Is her calm personality an advantage or is it really a disadvantage?

Dear Mum –
Lucky you! Many parents would love to have this problem! But your question points out that there are two sides to everything. You are right in thinking that, as your child grows older, you might need to help her not settle for "good enough" when she's capable of more.

Keep in mind that you're viewing her easy temperament through your own more challenging one. Let your partner's opinions balance your own so you avoid jumping to conclusions about your daughter. She needs to develop along her own path. Best wishes!

Sleep Training The Difficult Child
The difficult child is the hardest to sleep train. My elder daughter has a difficult temperament and was hard to train, so I know firsthand what you're going through if you have a Difficult Child too.

When sleep training a difficult child choose your sleep training technique with care. I have found that cry-it-out techniques, including the controlled crying of the Ferber method, don't work with this temperament. Remember that the Difficult Child wants what he wants when he wants it and is willing to persist until he gets it. I have heard of Difficult Children crying for up to six hours with the cry-it-out method!

If you have a difficult child, take a look at some of the no cry sleep training techniques. These techniques provide guidance that is gradually withdrawn as the child becomes more able to take responsibility for herself.

Sleep Training The Slow-To-Warm-Up Child
The Slow-To-Warm-Up Child is a bit in the middle when it comes to sleep training. You may find it difficult to get started with the sleep training, but when you do you'll see results fairly quickly.

You may find that cry-it-out techniques only make your child more anxious and clingy than she was before and that more gradual methods work better or you may find that cry-it-out works just fine. No-cry techniques may work well or they may only stretch out the process. With the Slow-To-Warm-Up Child, you'll need to feel your way and pay attention to what works best for your child.

Make sure you're not training the Slow-To-Warm-Up Child during a stage of separation anxiety. Between eight and 12 months is the hardest stage for sleep training any baby but especially hard for the Slow-To-Warm-Up Child.

Once your Slow-To-Warm-Up Child accepts sleep training, you will find he is a reliable sleeper. But, any disruption in the routine or detour for teething or illness may put things back to the beginning. Your patience and support at that point should restore sleep pretty quickly.

Sleep And Temperament Down The Road

Temperament isn't just a "baby thing" - it defines your child's preset condition now and throughout life. So when sleep issues recur because of illness, travel, or for seemingly no reason at all, you'll again want to take into consideration your child's temperament in helping her solve this problem.

When your child's sleep gets off track, try the same sleep-training technique you used successfully at the start to get your child's sleep back to normal. It will never take so long to get back on track as the initial sleep training took if you start getting back on track as soon as you can. Don't let the "new" not-so-good pattern become a habit.

Chapter Three
Creating Routines That Work

A lot about going to sleep happens long before we crawl into bed. Research has shown that light levels in the hour before bedtime help or hinder nodding off. So does screen time (in part because of the light these give off).

Because falling asleep depends on body chemistry, anything a person can do to trigger the timely secretion of sleep hormones prior to bedtime will contribute to a good night's sleep. One of the things a person can do is teach her body to respond to a go-to-bed routine.

Of course, this applies to children too.

Having a consistent go-to-bed routine - both for nighttime and naptime - will help your child settle. Because her body has picked up the cues, the sleep hormone melatonin is activated and sleepiness ensues. In addition, having a consistent routine makes it easier for you to stay consistent in your sleep training. As I've said before, consistency matters.

But here's something you might not have thought about: your child's go-to-bed routine is part of a larger *daily* routine. Having a daily routine will help your child sleep well. So let's start there.

The Daily Routine

Your daily routine can be whatever works for you and your family. It doesn't really matter if you like to get up at 6 am or 9 am, or if you want your child to go down for the night at 7 pm or 10 pm. What matters most is that each day follows the same pattern. You need a routine. That's what the word "routine" means, after all. It's what happens, over and over.

Some modern moms and dads resist a routine. They pride themselves on being ready for anything at a moment's notice. For them, "routine" means "dull." They hate the idea that their lives are dictated by the needs of little kids, instead of the little kids adapting to the whims of their parents. If this is you, then you may skip over this chapter. It will be here if you need something to read in the wee hours of the night when your child's sleep struggles keep both of you awake.

But even if you don't think you stick to a daily routine the chances are you do. Routine comes naturally to us humans. You eat three meals a day more than likely around the same time each day. You go to bed around the same time and get up at about the same time every day. The body's natural rhythms ensure that, even without a clock to go by, you do the same things every day at about the same times.

Having a routine for your child doesn't have to be restrictive. I'm not talking about having to be home all day or never being able to leave the house anywhere near a naptime. Your routine can be as structured as you want it to be. What's important is to

52

have some sort of routine. To get that it helps to follow some guidelines.

Wake-Up Time

Wake-up time should be the same daily, even on those days your child seems to want to sleep in. Yes, I know that the thought of waking up a sleeping child is not what you had in mind, but it really is beneficial. Let me explain.

When we are on a routine we want to go to sleep after about the same number of hours after we got up. Therefore if your child sleeps an extra hour in the morning, his morning nap will be an hour late, as will his afternoon nap, as will his bedtime! Then, because of the late bedtime, the following morning your child's wake-up time again will be later than usual - later than what used to be "usual" anyway. This may not seem like such a bad thing at first - 10 am, how lovely! - but I guarantee that before you know it going down to sleep for the night at 10 PM will become equally habitual - and not so lovely.

Set a wake-up time that results in a decent go-to-bed time and maintain that (yes, even on the weekends!) as part of your daily routine.

Of course, realistically, you want a bit of a lie-in on Saturday and Sunday. Remember, though, if you keep your child in bed an extra 30 minutes, to take that 30 minutes from a nap that day. Don't push bedtime half an hour later!

Dear Rebecca -
At 21 months we just weaned my son (2 days ago). I noticed he doesn't go down as easily because he's not calm enough, so we're looking for a new calming bedtime routine. We have always read books but now he won't sit still long enough to get calm without a pacifier.

When I was nursing I used to give him the pacifier in the crib as incentive to get in, so I would prefer not to give one prior. What do you recommend for a good nighttime routine now that nursing isn't part of it?

Dear Mum -
You can have some quiet playtime as part of the bedtime routine. Avoid noisy, flashing toys. Natural materials are perfect. The routine needs to be at least 30 minutes long.

You can start by getting ready for bed, have some playtime, milk in a cup or sippy cup, brush teeth, book, song and then in to bed.

It usually takes at least 3 nights for things to settle down when making changes. Best wishes!

Nap Time And Bed Time

Sleep time should be the same time daily.

When your child goes to sleep - both for naps during the day and at night - at the same time each day, her circadian rhythm is regulated. "Circadian rhythm" is the ticking of the child's internal body clock. When you keep sleep times consistent, your child will begin to get sleepy at the same times during the day and in the evening, making it easier for her to fall asleep. You also know that she will be ready for sleep, which makes it easier for you to sleep train.

Keeping a careful routine of awake and asleep times makes sure your child is getting enough sleep throughout the day and avoids over tiredness and overstimulation. Being overtired makes falling asleep almost impossible. There is actually a window of time when a sleepy person can fall asleep. Bypass that window, though, and the person gets a "second wind." Your child may seem to be running on fumes - crabby, nasty fumes - but still motoring full tilt. It seems to be a design flaw to me. You would think the more tired your child is the better she will sleep. That's just not the case. Delay naptime or bedtime at your peril!

Mealtimes

Mealtimes also should be at the same time daily. Both sleep and digestion depend on chemistry so keeping a routine for meals allows these body systems to mesh. Much like sleep we want to try for mealtimes at the same time each day.

Tweak The Daily Routine First

When I work with families I always start by tweaking the daily routine. By making some changes to your child's daily routine you can really have a positive impact on their night sleep.

I was recently working with a family whose eight-month old was waking as many as eight times a night. Obviously the parents were exhausted. We started by making some changes to the daily routine. We make sure that their daughter wasn't getting overtired or overstimulated before we tried to get her down for a nap. We ensured she wasn't napping too much or too little throughout the day. We adjusted the feed and meal times.

Within two weeks the little girl had gone from waking around eight times a night to waking just twice. She would feed quickly and then go back down to sleep without a fuss.

This is with only making some changes to the daily routine. We didn't change anything else!

When we tweak the routine and a child adjusts his night sleep, we don't need to do as much work at night compared to if we'd started straight away with the sleep training during the night.

Some Sample Routines

Here are some routines that have worked well for my client families. See if one of them seems to fit your child and your situation.

(The nap times on the sample schedules are when you want to your child to be sleeping or actively trying to get to sleep. They don't include any go-to-sleep routine. Start your nap routine 10 or 15 minutes before hand and start your wind down to the nap routine 10 or 15 minutes before that. More on nap and bedtime routines in a little bit.)

The Every-3-Hours Routine. This routine is appropriate for a baby younger than 6 months. The feedings are part of this schedule and awake time is shorter than nap time.

7:00 am	Wake
7:30 am	Playtime
8:30 am	Nap
10:00 am	Wake
10:30 am	Playtime
11:30 am	Nap
1:00 pm	Wake
1:30 pm	Playtime
2:30 pm	Nap
4:00 pm	Wake
4:30 pm	Playtime

5:30 pm or 6:00 pm	Short nap as needed
7:00 pm	Begin bedtime routine
7:30 pm	Bedtime

The Every-4-Hours Routine. This routine is similar to the 3-Hour routine, but both the awake times and the nap times are a bit longer. This routine might suit an infant between 4 and 9 months old, depending on the child.

7:00 am	Wake
7:30 am	Playtime
9:00 am	Nap
11:00 am	Wake
11:30 am	Playtime
1:00 pm	Nap
3:00 pm	Wake
3:30 pm	Playtime
5:00 pm or 6:00 pm	Nap if needed
7:00 pm	Begin bedtime routine
7:30 pm	Bedtime

The 2 – 3 – 4 Routine. This routine works really well for children from 6 to 18 months old who eat at more-or-less family meal times and who are still taking two naps a day. The idea with this routine is that your child is initially awake for 2 hours in the morning before going down for a nap. He is then awake for 3 hours after waking before going down for a second nap and is finally up for 4 hours before going to bed for the night. Two, then three, then four.

Children will stay on this schedule until they're ready to drop down to one nap.

Here is an example.

7 am	Wake up and play
9 am	Nap
10 am	Playtime
1 pm	Nap
3 pm	Wake up and play
6:30 pm	Start the bedtime routine
7 pm	Bedtime

Alternatively your child can take two 1 ½-hour naps instead of the naps shown here.

This routine can be adapted to your own acceptable wake up and bedtime (starting and ending on the 6s or 8s, for example).

Adjusting the Wake-Up Time

Your favorite wake-up time may be quite different from your child's natural wake-up time. Unfortunately, you can't really change this rhythm and you may need to make some compromise. Have reasonable expectations. Eventually your child will sleep in longer and adapt to your preferred schedule but this may take a while - a year or two.

Sleep Routines

The Go-To-Bed Routine

It's hard for children, no matter how young, to go from playing to sleep in a matter of minutes. There are some children who will sleep anytime, anywhere (usually it's an Easy Child who can manage this). But the majority of children will need some help winding down and getting ready for sleep. Establishing a dependable pattern that leads up to bedtime is a way to signal your child and your child's body chemistry that it's time to get sleepy.

Here's a sample routine to try.

- Dinner is the signal for the evening wind-down. No rough-housing or loud play after dinner.
- Keep the lights dim (or off) in the house after dinner and let the evening slowly creep in.
- Prep the child's bedroom by dimming the lights.
- Serve milk or bottle if desired or necessary.
- If you do a nightly bath (and if your child doesn't find baths too exciting) have a quiet wash.
- Jammies on.
- Teeth brushed.
- Read 2 or 3 books. Let your child choose the books if he wishes but always end on the same book, if you can.
- If you like, sing a song or two. Let your child choose the songs but always end on the same song.

- Tuck the child into bed with whatever lovey is required.
- If you use a mobile, quiet music or white noise machine, turn it on now.
- Dim the lights to dark as you tiptoe out the room.

Whatever works for you is fine. Just do things the very same way every night. The routine will likely run about 45 minutes.

The Naptime Routine

A naptime routine serves the same function as the go-to-bed routine: it gets the child and the child's body chemistry ready for sleep. A nap routine needs to be between 10 and 15 minutes long to really be effective, so plan this into your day. Also, remember to not start anything exciting or interesting in the 10 to 15 minutes ahead of the naptime routine. Make the entire half hour or so ahead of nap a time more calm than the rest of the day.

As part of your child's naptime routine, do exactly the same things in exactly the same order for every naptime that happens at home. For example:

- Go to your child's room and close the shades.
- Quiet play in the child's room is a nice option.
- Sit down together and read a book 2 or three times. You may want to finish with the same book each time; that way the child will know when books are over. If you like, a 12 months and older child might choose the books. If

Dear Rebecca -
My 4 month-old's naps are getting even shorter (often just 25 minutes- down from 45), but if I let her fall asleep in my arms she'll be out for an hour and half or even 2 hours. I've tried making her crib cozier and warmer, but that doesn't seem to make a difference.

Is there anything to do? I've been letting her "grow out" of these short naps for probably 7 weeks with almost no change.

Dear Mum -
Make sure that you are getting her down at the right time (after about 1½ hours to 2 hours of awake time) and that she's not over stimulated. Most short naps are due to over stimulation.

You can avoid over stimulation by spending between 15 and 20 minutes getting ready for the nap. Spend 5 or 10 minutes as a wind down (just walking around quietly) and the other 10 as a nap routine (same things in the same place in the same order).

If this doesn't help you'll want to teach her how to fall asleep independently if she already doesn't.

Good luck!

- you can let her feel as in control as possible over as many of the negotiable things as possible, naptime will go a little smoother.
- Sing a song or two. Again, the 12 months and older child might choose the songs. End on the same song every naptime.
- Tuck the child into bed, along with whatever stuffed toy or lovey is necessary.

As your child gets more and more used to this routine, she will begin to unwind and relax as soon as you go into her room.

Try to get at least one nap at home each day. Napping at home in the dark will always provide your child with better sleep than napping-on-the-go.

Variations To Try When Things Don't Work

Special Technique: The Walking Wind-Down
Some children, especially Difficult Children, just cannot calm themselves for sleep in an "ordinary" wind-down. This child is still keyed up, still motoring, even after you've dimmed the lights and read some stories.

If this is your child, try the Walking Wind-Down. Before launching your go-to-bed routine, take 10 or 15 minutes to just walk around the house with your little person in your arms. Walk slowly and rhythmically. Be quiet and soothing. Help your child settle and relax. When you've achieved baby-calm,

63

proceed with your usual routine but keep things slow and soft.

Routine Reset #1

Sometimes the routine stops working. As your child becomes more physically capable, he may begin to act out a little during the routine, running around instead of looking at books, for instance.

If your child does this it's a good idea to change one aspect of the routine. For example, you may read books while sitting on the floor, instead of on a chair, or you might sing songs before you read the books. Changing the routine slightly seems to keep toddlers on their toes and interested in what will come next.

Change the routine only when you really need to but before you become exasperated. Remember that calmness and consistency are the keys.

Routine Reset #2

Sometimes the routine gets out of whack, not because the child gets silly about it but because you've been traveling, someone's been sick, or you've just run into a string of disruptions that all happen at naptime or bedtime. This stuff happens.

Just go back to your established routine, whatever that is. Stick to it like glue. Most likely, your child will fall back into the old rhythm in a day or two. If not, recheck your daily schedule and see if that needs a bit of a tweak.

The Pay-Off

Children who have a consistent bedtime routines established by the time they are three months old are more likely to be able to get themselves asleep and back to sleep without help. Your routine is an essential part of the sleep training plan. In fact, it might be all your child needs!

Chapter Four
Where To Sleep

It seems so simple. You bring the baby home and put her down to sleep. Maybe you've decorated a nursery and outfitted it with a crib. Maybe you bought a new home *just so* the baby could have a room of her own. And now you're not so sure.

And then... after a few years, you're ready for a change. No matter where you settled on sleeping your baby now it's time for her to graduate to a different location or a different bed. And there's some resistance to that.

Figuring out where your child will sleep seems like such a simple thing but it's complicated with safety issues, with issues of attachment and convenience, and issues of your own sleep needs. As your child grows older she will have her own opinions and they might conflict with yours - opinions that may depend upon her temperament. So what's the answer?

When it's bedtime in your household where do the children go to sleep?

Where To Sleep A Newborn

You have some choices here, choices that might have surfaced only on your baby's first night at home when the fantasy you had of your child's sleep routine was rudely interrupted by reality. The choices are basically "alone" or "with you." If you choose "with you," then there are two more choices: in a bed of his own or in your bed.

We'll walk through these options but first here's something to keep in mind: whatever you think you're going to do before your baby is born might be different from what you actually decide to do once he's in your arms. You might think you'll co-sleep with your baby only to find it just doesn't work for you and your partner. You might think you'll never in a million years allow your baby to sleep in your bed, only to find that having him near is the one way you can get any sleep yourself.

Sleep is very personal and it's not easy to predict how sleeping with another, very dependent and precious person in the house is going to affect you. So keep your options open. Don't box yourself in but recognize that your first idea might not be the one you stick with.

Another thing to keep in mind is this: whatever you decide, your partner must be part of the decision. Again, stay flexible and understand that the first decision you reach together might not be the final one. Your baby's needs are important and your needs are important too. But your partner's needs also are important and what sounded good on paper might not play out well in real life. If the family's sleep arrangements aren't working for everyone, they're not working.

Don't feel pressured into one sleeping arrangement or another by your family or your friends. Every family is different and every family must make its own decision. I didn't co-sleep either of my children. I am such a light sleeper that I would wake whenever the baby moved. I put my daughters in a bassinet next to our bed.

With these caveats in mind, let's take a look at having baby sleep "with you."

Co-Sleeping

Co-sleeping is the original sleeping method. As its advocates point out, around the world and down through history most babies have slept in a bed with at least their mothers, if not with their entire families.

An obvious advantage of co-sleeping with a breast-fed baby is that one needn't get out of bed to nurse. You don't even need to fully wake up. Co-sleeping advocates believe that frequent nighttime on-demand nursing is better for newborns than scheduled feeds and helps them sleep through the night almost immediately from birth.

But other studies find that co-sleeping infants sleep more lightly than own-bed infants and that their mothers (and fathers) may find it difficult to sleep soundly also. Infants can be very noisy and wiggly! So the choice to use co-sleeping really comes down to preference: is this the experience you and your partner want?

69

If so, then there are a few things to consider. First in places and times where co-sleeping is traditional, bedding is different from bedding in most American homes today. Our mattresses are softer and thicker. Our beds are higher off the floor. Our blankets and duvets our heavier and more plush. These differences mean that to co-sleep safely, you must sleep more like traditional families from the past and less like modern day people.

Follow these guidelines:

- Make certain there is no gap between your bed and the wall or between your mattress and headboard where an infant could be trapped.
- Choose a firm mattress.
- Cuddly though it seems, the baby should not be placed between parents, where a valley can form to trap the child.
- The baby should sleep on top of the covers and should never use a pillow.
- An infant should not share your bed if you're also sharing your bed with other children or with family pets.

In addition, the adults sharing the bed with an infant may not have been drinking or using drugs, including prescription medication or over-the-counter sleep aids that might impair a parent's ability to be aware of what's going on.

Obviously, the risk of an adult rolling onto an infant exists only in a co-sleeping situation. This doesn't mean that co-sleeping is more dangerous than other sleep arrangements but that this particular danger is unique to co-sleeping. With care in choosing bedding and in organizing the way the bed is shared, you can minimize this risk.

It should be pointed out that your infant is not safe sleeping in an adult's bed by himself. So even if you co-sleep with your baby, you will need a crib or bassinet for your baby's naps.

In Your Room But In Another Bed

Many parents want their newborn nearby in the first few weeks but not so nearby as in the parents' own bed. In fact, experts suggest that this is the safest course for the first six months. To do this just place the child's crib in the parents' room.

Doing this makes it simpler to hear the child when she wakes in the night, though it also makes it simpler to be awakened by your baby's normal sleeping noises. You may find yourself lying awake, just listening to her breathe, which is not such a good thing (though it does reduce the risk of SIDS). On the other hand, the child is conveniently placed for night feeds. When you decide that she's old enough to sleep in her own room, it's simple to just move the crib. Your child doesn't need to get used to sleeping on her own, since she'll have been doing this since birth.

Of course, there are safety measures to take into account when sleeping a child in a crib. We'll talk about those next.

In A Crib In The Baby's Own Room
Putting your baby to bed in his own room is another possibility. Doing this sets early the permanent sleeping arrangement most parents want for their children, so there is no need for a transition later. (Remember experts suggest you not do this until your baby is at least six months old.)

Also, when your baby sleeps down the hall, parents have more privacy, for reading in bed with the lights on or for doing other things in bed, maybe with the lights off. Freedom from baby during the night hours is very welcome for many parents and is something to consider.

On the other hand, trekking into another room for midnight feedings can definitely be a chilly and lonely experience.

Safe Sleeping In A Crib

No matter what sleeping arrangement you choose for nighttime, you will need to use a crib or bassinet for daytime naps. It's just not safe for a baby to sleep alone in a "real bed." So everyone needs to know about crib safety (most of this applies to bassinets, cradles, and other sleeping locations. The idea is to reduce the danger of suffocation, SIDS, and strangulation. This is important stuff.

Buy A New Crib
Despite the charm of antique cribs, including the crib you yourself slept in as a child, using an old crib can

be very dangerous. Old cribs have widely-spaced bars that can catch a child's head, they may have gaps between the mattress and the crib frame, they may have loosened bolts that can cause
the crib to collapse or they even may be coated in lead paint. Standards for crib safety have increased so that many old cribs, including all cribs with drop-sides, have been labeled unsafe and even have been recalled by their manufacturers.

Unless you are certain a used crib complies with all recent safety requirements, buy a new one. Cribs do not need to be fancy. They just need to be safe.

Use No Bedding
You may have received beautiful linens for your nursery from well-meaning friends. Use only the fitted bottom sheet and a mattress pad (if you like) that fits snugly under the bottom sheet. If you received top sheets use them to make curtains!

Don't use bumpers, pillows, or blankets. Lay that gorgeous handmade quilt from Aunt Betty on the family room floor as a play space. Don't put it in the baby's bed and don't drape it stylishly over the side. If you're worried about your child being cold in the night, dress him in fleecy footed jammies or a sack-style bunting.

Keep crib toys and stuffed animals to an absolute minimum. Babies under six months old don't really care about having toys in the bed and it's best to not include them at all.

Dear Rebecca -
I currently co-sleep with Lucy, who will be 10 weeks old tomorrow. When is an appropriate time to start moving her to the bassinet that sits next to my bed? I want to then transition her into a crib in her own room.

The co-sleeping is going good and she is already on a bit of a sleeping schedule - going to bed around 8 or 9 PM then waking up around 4 or 5 AM for feeding, then back to sleep until 7 or 8 AM.

Dear Mum -
Don't worry just yet. There's plenty of time. But... you may want to pop Lucy in her bassinet for her nap or at the beginning of the night, just to see how it goes.

If she doesn't take too well to that, you can just let her have some awake or playtime in there. Even a few minutes is good. You can also do the same with the crib.

The mattress should be firm. Don't be tricked into buying a soft, pillow-top-type crib mattress. Firm is the only safe option.

Check For Safety Round About
Make certain that no cords of any kind are within reach of the crib. This includes cords for curtains and shades, cords hanging from a mobile, and electrical cords. If you hang a mobile over the crib, be certain it is well out of your baby's reach and is in no danger of falling into the crib. Make sure that wall decorations are also secure. If you use a baby monitor, position it well out of the crib. Even though it might have a video option, all you really need (if you need a monitor at all) is audio.

Keep in mind that electric appliances, like a baby monitor, HEPA filter, heater or fan, can change the electromagnetic fields in the room. The effects of electrical interference are not fully understood but constitute a risk that probably can easily be avoided. Unless there is a compelling reason for using electrical equipment in a baby's room, the safest plan is to not use it at all. This includes baby monitors, which were not "necessary" before they were invented.

Get The Bedroom Ready For Sleep
Whether you use the crib just for naps or for naps and night sleeping you may want blackout drapes to shut out sunlight and street lamps. If your home seems noisy or if you live on a busy street, you might also want a white noise machine or a CD player. A radio tuned to static also works.

Make certain the temperature in the nursery is neither too hot on summer afternoons nor too cold on frigid winter nights. Your infant will sleep better if the room temperature is between 65 and 70° F. Watch what you're dressing your child in. You want to make sure he doesn't overheat.

However, you also don't want to try to move a child who's fallen asleep in your arms into a cold bed. Doing that is like setting off an alarm clock. So warm the crib using a heating pad set on low for a few minutes before putting the child down. Just taking the edge off the coolness of the bottom sheet may help your infant remain asleep. Please remember to remove the heating pad before you place your child in the crib or bassinet, though. Never leave a heating pad, hot water bottle or any other device in the crib with your child.

Clear the clutter. Remember that you will be navigating your child's room in the dark, when you're not fully awake, and maybe when your vision is blocked by a screaming, flailing infant. Make sure the path from the door to the crib presents no tripping hazards. Pick up the toys, keep chairs and ottomans out of the way and make sure the edges of any rugs are firmly taped down.

For the complete effect include the smell of you. Wearing the crib sheet before you put it in the crib will impart the sheet with your scent and help your baby feel extra secure. This is especially helpful if you're making a transition from co-sleeping to sleeping alone. Just place the crib sheet under your shirt or sweater against her skin for a short period before you put it in the crib.

Back To Sleep
Remember that no matter what your grandmother says, place your child on his back. Deaths from SIDS have fallen significantly since parents started following this simple rule. Yes, babies tend to fall asleep quicker on their tummies. Yes, babies are more liable to startle when they sleep on their backs. But knowing you've done everything you can to avoid SIDS is worth the effort that putting children down on their backs can require.

Once your child can reliably roll from back to tummy and from tummy to back, you can quit trying to micro-manage his sleeping position. You may still put him to sleep on his back - he will be used to it by this time (by around six months). But if he turns over in his sleep or before falling asleep there's no need to move him onto his back again. No need to worry.

Sleeping Two Kids To A Room

Maybe there are two (or more) children sleeping in the "kids' room." What then? You'll likely find your own path but here are some suggestions.

Children Of The Same Age
If you have twins, you will likely put them to sleep in the same room. Most parents of multiples find things work best when each child has her own crib or bassinet. This reduces the chances that children will

Dear Rebecca -
Any tips on transitioning at 2 1/2 year old and a
nine-month-old into sharing a bedroom?

Dear Dad -
Does your nine-month-old sleep through the
night? It's helpful – but not necessary – if he
does.

You may want to do your children's bedtime
routine separately for a little while. Get the nine-
month-old down to sleep first. Around 20 minutes
later the baby will be into a deep sleep and you
can get the 2 1/2-year-old to bed then.

You may want to use some white noise to begin
with, just to see if they're going to disturb each
other. But children - especially toddlers - sleep
quite deeply and may not disturb each other.

Try it and see how things go. You can always
tweak if an issue arises. But like anything else,
being committed to the new arrangement
yourself is half the battle!

disturb each other or that one may roll onto another one. It also makes it easier to nurse each child without waking the other.

Children Of Different Ages

If your infant will share a room with an older sib, try to set up an area for a crib, chair for nursing, and table for bottles, a flashlight, and so on that is separate from the older child's area. Most toddlers and preschoolers sleep soundly and are not bothered by a crying baby in the night. They sleep blissfully through most anything. Depending on the age and mobility of the older child, you may need to make certain the baby cannot be poked or prodded by her sibling or "cared for" in ways that are well-intentioned but not altogether safe.

You might start both children off in the same room - maybe the room nearest your own - with plans to move the older child to a new "big boy" or "big girl" room in a little while. We'll talk about helping your toddler or preschool make this transition in a later chapter.

Temperament And Sleeping Location

Does temperament matter in your choice of where to put your baby to sleep? Yes. But at the time you'll be making your first decision here - when your baby is anywhere from 24 to 72 hours old - you likely won't know your child's temperamental predisposition yet.

Dear Rebecca -
How and when do you transition from a crib to a toddler bed? Our daughter is 21 months and sleeps really great in her crib - she has never shown any interest in climbing out of it. We have baby #2 coming in August who will eventually need the crib, but we can put that off for several months while he/she is in a bassinet.

Dear Dad -
You will want to have a little while between your daughter coming out of the crib and new baby going in. Your daughter doesn't want to think that she was moved out so the baby can go in HER crib! 2 or 3 weeks should be plenty long enough.

I would be very tempted to leave her in the crib until you really need to make the move. A child who has the freedom to get out of a bed will make the most of this freedom, especially when there are changes within the family.

Best wishes!

So you might not know your child's temperament in time to make this choice. Your child's response to your choice, though, might help you know his temperament.

The Easy Child may sleep readily no matter what arrangement you choose. The Difficult Child might struggle to sleep anywhere. He may keep everyone awake when co-sleeping and may find himself sleeping in a crib down the hall fairly quickly. The Slow-To-Warm-Up Child may have some difficulty with sleep at first but then may settle in whatever situation you've chosen, only to be less happy with any change. She may co-sleep well but not sleep happily in a crib for naps. She may have difficulty at two months moving from your room to a room of her own.

So, while temperament will have an effect here, it doesn't help much to try to base your decision on it. Instead, you get to live and learn.

Everyone wants the best for baby and everyone wants a good night's sleep. Try to arrange the sleeping situation so a good night's sleep can be had by all.

Chapter Five
Sleep Training Methods

Now that you understand your child's temperament just a bit better, how can you apply this to sleep training? Isn't that what you really want to know: How do you do this?

There are several methods promoted by different experts. All of these have been in use in one form or another by parents and babysitters throughout human history. One writer or another may attach a cute name to this technique or that one but there are just a few basic strategies. One of these is right for you and your child.

Be certain, before you start thinking about sleep training that your child is at least three or four months old and that you have already established a daytime routine and are working on a naptime and bedtime routine. Of course, you need more sleep but be sure to do things in the right order even so.

Let's start, though, by talking about basic truths that apply to every technique. After that, we'll talk about the techniques themselves.

Basic Sleep Training Truths

Start On Friday night
I always suggest starting any sleep training on a Friday night. That way if you're up a lot through the night you and your partner can tag team nap through the

weekend. And don't plan on going out on the Saturday night you start sleep training. Make sleep training your weekend project and see if by Sunday night you've made a bit of progress.

Commit To A Strategy

After you've thought hard about your child's temperamental presets and you've figured out which sleep training technique is best for your child and for you, commit to it. Sleep training, by definition, doesn't achieve results immediately... the word "training" means you work on this over a period of time. So you've got to give the method you choose a chance. You should begin to see progress within three or four nights.

Be Consistent

You really must be consistent. Understand the technique you've chosen and follow it to the letter. Don't give up or give in.

Really, inconsistency isn't fair to your child. It's not fair to make your child feel frustrated (as sleep training almost inevitably does) and then give in after his frustration reaches a peak. This would be very annoying if it happened to you and it makes sleep training take much longer than it should. Your child will think he has to be frustrated for a long time before he finally gets what he wants.

Studies done on sleep training techniques have found that no technique works better than any other as long *as you are consistent*. Consistency is key.

You also don't want your child thinking if she cries long enough the "good" parent will come and give her what she wants. Make sure both parents are on the same page.

Get On The Same Page

It's important that one parent doesn't assume the other parent knows what's going on or doesn't have an opinion about sleep training. Iron things out before you start. Discuss what you want your goals to be, what sleep training technique you want to use and exactly what you both need to do and when. You will reach your goals quicker if you are working together as a team.

Tag Team

There's no reason to sleep train by yourself. This is a family project. Enlist the help of your child's other parent and take turns at 10- or 20-minute intervals at bedtime. Take turns if your child wakes in the night. If you're on your own, get a friend to help out - make an evening of it. Sleep training is so much easier if you have someone else who can take a turn and someone else who shares in just how hard this can be.

Stay Calm

Try to remain calm and relaxed through the whole process. This isn't easy, I know. Babies' cries are *supposed* to be upsetting - it's Nature's way of making sure someone is paying attention. But babies also are wired to pick up on emotions around them. If you are stressed and tense, your child will be stressed and tense too.

Talking quietly and reassuring your child will help keep you calm. Don't worry if your child can't hear you because he's crying so loudly and don't try to talk over him, as it will quickly become a yelling contest. Detach yourself from your own frustration and anger. Concentrate on staying quiet and calm.

Try Ear Plugs

This seems funny, doesn't it? But ear plugs really can help. Find ear plugs that don't block all sounds but just dampen things a bit. Anything that keeps you calmer and more serene is a good thing.

Try Music

Lullabies are for parents as much as for children. Sing to your child any quiet song or put on some quiet, calming music - calming for you - at your child's bedtime. Hum or sing along. Any music will work so pick something you like and let yourself get in the groove.

Take A Time Out

Sometimes you just need a timeout. If you're in your child's room trying to help her fall asleep and she's continuing to struggle and you're getting more and more frustrated, it can all get a bit much- even if you and your partner tag team and if you're using earplugs and you're singing as quietly but as hard as you can. You can reach the end of your endurance. It's okay. Give yourself a timeout.

Make sure your child is safe and just leave the room. Try to find someplace where you can't hear her cry, take a few deep breaths and get yourself back to calm. Just a minute or two will help you to reset yourself. If you need to, call your mother or call a friend. Make a quick Facebook post. Get some support.

Needing to take a timeout doesn't mean you're not a good parent. It's fine and perfectly normal for a child's cry to begin to grate the brain after a while. You just don't want to lose it completely and start to scream at your child or - heaven help us! - shake your child.

It's okay to take a time out.

Moderate Your Expectations

Night One may not be quite as bad as you thought it would be but Night Two will be more like you expected: it will be a bit worse than Night One. By Night Three there should be some real improvement. Within a week you should be feeling pretty good about all this.

But your life will not magically transform. You may still have difficulty sleeping, since you might keep waking to check on your child ("Can she possibly be all right? I haven't heard from her in two hours!")

And the rosy glow will not last. Unfortunately you can expect a regression around a week after either starting the sleep training or around a week after you've seen results from the sleep training. Understand that this is just part of the process and it doesn't mean that the sleep training didn't "take" or that there's something really wrong.

The best way to deal with regression is just as you did the first night of sleep training. You're a pro at this by

Dear Rebecca –
Our son is 9 months old, and cosleeps with us. We don't normally go to sleep till 11 pm or midnight so I'm worried he is not getting enough sleep since we get up around 8:30 am regardless of what time he goes down. I've tried getting him to sleep earlier - around 8 pm - but he wakes up within an hour and freaks out that we left him there. Also, he is crawling now, so I'm afraid to leave him on the bed alone. So, is there a way to get him to sleep a full 11-12 hours without us going to bed at 8-9 pm? I've also heard that sleeping from 7 pm-7 am is more beneficial for brain development than sleeping 11 pm-11 am? Is this true?

Dear Mum –
I don't think the time of the sleep matters, 11 pm here is 7 pm somewhere!

When you are trying to begin the night really early your son just treats it as a nap. You can gradually bring bedtime earlier and earlier. Get him down to sleep around 15 minutes earlier for a couple of nights and then another 15 minutes earlier a couple of nights later, repeat, repeat until he's at the new bedtime.

It's not safe to have him crawling around the bed without anyone else there. You can just have a mattress on the floor and make the room very safe. There are many no-cry sleep training techniques you can try if you're ready to teach independent sleep skills.

now so just pretend you're starting over. Regression usually lasts one or two nights. Don't give up and don't switch to a new method.

If your child was an older baby when you launched sleep training he will have a stronger habit to break and regression may last longer. The longer the habit, the more nights of regression. Just don't despair. You know what you need to do.

Read Your Baby's Cries

Not all cries are created equal. A fussy, low-decibel cry doesn't need much attention. Humming, fretting, and mumbling need absolutely no attention at all (these sounds usually mean sleep is just around the corner!). But the Mommy-I-Need-You-Now cry is your summons. This one you should attend to.

The Mommy-I-Need-You-Now cry (MINYN) indicates your child has crossed the border from ordinarily unhappy to out of control. Infants cannot walk themselves back from this emotional cliff and need your help to calm themselves. If you do not intervene, they will sob until they fall asleep from exhaustion, which is not a good thing. Recognize the MINYN cry and be ready to step in to guide your child back to solid ground.

Sleeping Training Methods

Let's walk through some of the most popular and useful strategies for helping children learn how to fall asleep on their own. Remember that some of these techniques are not right for you and your child. Some of these techniques will not suit your child's temperament or your own inclinations. Your job here is to think about each of these in the context of what you know about your child's presets. One of these methods will be right for you.

I'm going to walk you through the popular methods you might have heard about. And, at the end, I'll let you in on my own favorite method, which I call "The Michi Method."

Cry-It-Out

This is what you think it is: you put the child down in his crib or bassinet, turn out the light, walk out the door, and let him cry himself to sleep. Some children cry for only a short time before settling down and for them this technique works fine. Other, more Difficult children, do not respond well and escalate their crying until they reach Mommy-I-Need-You-Now, sometimes in only a minute or two.

There is no evidence that Cry-It-Out interferes with attachment so long as it's part of an otherwise supportive family environment. Many parents, though, find this technique difficult to implement, since it requires more unshakeable resolve than they can muster. Inconsistency will ruin the effectiveness of Cry-It-Out (just as it ruins every method), so don't start this if you think you won't be able to follow through or if your partner objects.

This method is most appropriate for an Easy Child. It is not appropriate for a Difficult Child and should be used with caution if your child is Slow-To-Warm-Up.

Modified Cry-It-Out

This method was popularized by Richard Ferber, in his book *Solve Your Child's Sleep Problems*. It's often called "The Ferber Method" or even "Ferberizing." It's an application of classic extinction methods developed by behavioral psychologists in the 20th century. In this method, crying is expected but it's time-limited. The crying time is gradually increased until the child learns to settle by herself.

Here's a typical schedule for Modified Cry-It-Out:

<u>Night One:</u> Put the baby to bed while she is still awake and leave the room. If she starts crying, let her be for about five minutes then comfort her for a short period *without* picking her up, rocking or feeding her. Then leave the room again.

If your baby cries again (as she probably will) wait for ten minutes before returning to comfort her (again, do not pick him up). The third time you leave the room, wait for fifteen minutes before responding if she cries.

Continue to wait for 15 minutes each time she cries until your baby falls asleep.

<u>Night Two:</u> For the second night, begin with letting your child cry for 10 minutes before attending to her, increasing next to 15 minutes and then to 20 minute intervals.

<u>Night Three:</u> Begin with waiting for 15 minutes of crying before going to your child (remember to not

pick her up!). Repeat this process until baby adapts to the sleeping habit.

Modified Cry-It-Out requires attention to the clock. You likely will find that using a timer helps here. It also assumes that your baby will soothe quickly when you go to her - an assumption that may not be true at all.

This method also works best for Easy babies and less well (or not at all) for Difficult babies. Slow-To-Warm-Up children might respond well to this method or might not.

Pat-The-Baby (for babies 3 to 6 months)
This gentle method ensures your baby is asleep before you leave the room. It's especially nice for very young babies. The key to making this method work is your ability to stay calm and quiet and very, very patient.

Swaddle your baby and lay him on his side. Make sure he can't roll onto his front by placing your hand on his back. Lean over the crib. Firmly pat your child's back. You need to shush just past his ear. Make the shhhhh long and drawn out. Don't shush right into the ear (wouldn't that be annoying?) but across it. Obviously this won't be simple if the baby is far away from your lips but just do the best you can without pulling your shoulder out of joint.

If your child doesn't settle, pick him up and hold him to you shoulder. When your baby has relaxed and his breathing becomes deeper, lay him back in the crib. Pat and shush again.

If he stays quiet, start to slow the patting to a stop but continue shushing for another 5 minutes. If all is still well, slow and stop the shushing. It can take up to 20 minutes for your child to fall fully asleep, so be patient. Your child is in a deep sleep when his eyes stop moving side to side, his breathing slows and becomes shallow, and his body relaxes.

Stay for a few minutes to see if he's fully asleep. There is a possibility he will jolt wake again. Restart the patting and shushing. If he cries then pick him up and start again.

This method is appropriate for babies of all temperaments.

Pat-The-Baby (for babies 6 to 8 months)
When your baby is a little older, you can try this variation on Pat-The-Baby. This version transfers a little of the responsibility for falling asleep to the child, while still keeping crying to a minimum.

When you go to put your child down to sleep for the night, do your usual nighttime routine. Lay your child down in the crib. Try to leave, though the chances are your child will get upset, roll over and sit up. She may even stand up!

Try soothing with your voice, but if that doesn't work pick her up. Hold your child in a horizontal position and soothe with your voice. If you prefer, you may soothe your child against your shoulder, but don't let her fall asleep there.

When she stops crying, immediately lay her back down, on her side facing away from you. Place a firm hand on her back and Reassure her that it's okay, talk to her reassuringly. Be soft, gentle, and persuasive. Rub your child's back, pat gently, or just maintain a gentle pressure. Use your voice a lot to reassure.

When your child seems to have settled, gradually withdraw your hand and back slowly away. Keep talking soothingly.

Your child may detect your departure. If she can stand, wait until she stands up, then lay her back down just as you did before. If your child doesn't stand yet but can sit up, wait until she sits up before restarting the process. Children may check what's going on and then settle themselves, so don't be too quick to come back to intervene. If your child is still swaddled, wait until you hear the Mommy I Need You Now Cry before picking her up.

If at any point in the process your child fights you (fidgeting in your arms, or rubbing her head against you) pop her in the crib. These are signs that she is trying to soothe herself.

If you are making the move to lay your child down and she begins to cry before you've even got her in the crib, continue to lay her down. You can pick her up straight away if you need to.

I've found this method is appropriate for children of any temperament.

Tippy-Toe-Out

In this method, you maintain a close presence but avoid picking up the child unless he really cries.

Start by positioning a chair next to the crib. Test out this chair ahead of time to make certain you can sit in it for a while with your hands through the bars and not strain your back doing it.

<u>Nights One through Three.</u> Lay your child in the crib close enough to reach him from your chair. Reach through the bars to touch your child gently and use your voice to soothe or even sing a song. Don't hold your child's hand or let him hold yours. It's fine to pat, but don't pat in a rhythm, since when you stop patting it will be more noticeable.

If your child stands up lay him straight down. Try not to pick him up, though if your child is really upset pick him up and remain over the crib.

Assuming your child settles, remain sitting in the chair until fully asleep (the child, not you!).

<u>Nights Four through Six</u>. Move the chair a little distance away from the crib. Put your child down as before and use the soothing sounds to help him settle. Try to remain in the chair as much as possible (this means you're not touching your child). If your child cries a little, try to remain seated and soothe first with your voice. When your child seems settled, stand quietly and tiptoe out.

Dear Rebecca –
My 10 month old has been waking up between 1:30 and 2:30 am almost nightly since he was 6 months. This waking typically lasts 1.5 hours but at about 2 am it's as long as 3 hours! Nothing works to get him back to sleep any faster. We've co-slept since birth, and he was a frequent nurser (every 2 hours) until 5 months when he was giving me a 5 hour stretch. Now he is waking every 90 min crying till I nurse him back to sleep, but won't nurse at the 2 am prolonged wake-up.

We've just begun trying to transition him to a crib by our bed and put him down drowsy but awake. It's been tough. Takes 2 hours for him to sleep this way. Any idea what we can do?

Dear Mum -
I think it may be time to stop co-sleeping full time. Drowsy but awake is a bit of a myth I think! Can you imagine being nice and drowsy and falling asleep and then being moved? I would be really mad! Teaching your child to fall asleep from wide awake is actually easier, though he will always need your help if he wakes more than just to " drowsy."

The habit of the long wake up will be broken with the sleep training. You have done some great preparation for sleep training. I don't think you will find it too hard.

<u>Nights Seven through Nine.</u> Move the chair further away, right up to the door if you can (but don't block your own exit!). Lay your child down as before and use your voice to soothe and reassure him. Intervene as little as possible and stay in the chair as much as possible. As soon as your child seems settled, tiptoe out.

This method works nicely with Easy and Slow-To-Warm-Up children and can work well with Difficult children also.

The Michi Method

Here's my favorite method that lets you use what you're comfortable with in any combination. You just remove one of your supports every fourth night until the child is settling on her own.

There are three keys to this method:
1. Respond immediately to a Mommy-I-Need-You-Now cry but not to fussing or whining;
2. Be hands-off until it's clear your child is getting sleepy;
3. Stay attuned to your child's preferences.

Oh, and remove one item every fourth night.

Here's how to do it.

When you go to put your child down to sleep for the night, do your usual nighttime routine. But do not nurse your child to sleep, or bounce, rock, or anything else. Just lay your child down in the crib.

Try to leave. Chances are your child will get upset, roll over and sit up. She may even stand up!

Try soothing with your voice. If that doesn't work and you hear the Mommy-I-Need-You-Now cry, pick her up. Soothe your child any way you can: you can bounce, rock, sing, talk, or whatever. But do not let her fall asleep on you. Hold her until she's calmed down, or the cry has changed from the MINYN cry. When her crying stops or becomes the mad or fussy cry lay her back in the crib. She will jump back up or get into a sitting position if she can. If she can't sit or stand yet she may kick her legs, roll around and generally carry on.

It's okay to talk to your child to help settle her, but only on the first few nights. After a night or two, be less "present" when your child seems to be avoiding sleep and talk only when she's settling and sleepy.

If (or when) your child gets upset again - and "upset" means only that you hear the Mommy-I-Need-You-Now cry, so wait for it! - you can again pick her up until she has soothed. Then put her back down.

You should lay your child down every 3 to 5 minutes, even if he doesn't need picking up. To lay a child down when he's standing, unclasp his hands from the crib rail, hold his hands and sit him back down onto his bottom. Twist him around on his bottom and lay him on his back. Don't pick him up and lay him back down if he's standing. Just lay him back down.

Repeat, repeat, and repeat until your child becomes sleepy and tired. You can tell when your child becomes tired as he doesn't jump up so quickly as before. When he's getting sleepy, he may just sit up or roll around, his cry can sound different, and he may start rubbing his head on the mattress.

This is your cue for keeping your hands on your child. You can rub his tummy, back or head. You can pat his back. You can sing or talk or shush. If you hear the MINYN cry, pick your child up and lay him back down as soon as he's settled a bit.

Remember: only pat or rub your child if he is showing signs of being sleepy. Do not do this if he is still fighting sleep.

If you are holding your child when he starts to rub his head on your shoulder, pop him into the crib. He is trying to get himself to sleep.

If your child begins to cry whilst you are placing her into the crib (again it needs to be the MINYN cry), continue to put her down and then pick her straight up again.

If your touch makes your child angry, you may want to pat and shush sparingly. The picking up and putting down can make your child just as mad. If that's the case, you'll want to do these as little as possible. Just stay next to the crib to help him with your voice and touch. Take your cues from your child.

Continue to pick up, put down and place your hands on your baby's back or side or head for as needed. Eventually your child will settle and fall asleep.

Gradually stop your support until you're sure your child is asleep. It's tempting to hurry out the door, but I suggest waiting in the room until your child is in to a deep sleep. You want to be in the room if he wakes up before he has got into that deep sleep, so you can help him back to sleep. If your child begins to come into a light sleep (if he moves or makes a noise) you can begin to help him again with your voice or with a gentle touch to help him settle into a deeper sleep.

If your child wakes during the night go through the same technique. Make sure you are only going to help them when the cry has got to the MINYN cry. There is a chance he will be able to get himself back to sleep if the cry is not loud and urgent. Some children can be awake for up to an hour before they get themselves back to sleep. This is fine and perfectly normal. They may cry a little (a mantra cry which is waa, waa, waa), quiet down for a minute or two, babble or talk for a while, cry again, and so on. Of course, you'll be awake, hearing all this, but don't intervene. It's important you only go to you to your child when the MINYN cry tells you you're really needed.

It is so important to be consistent with this and any sleep training technique. It can take up to an hour (sometimes even more) for your child to fall asleep on the first night, and the same amount of time during the night. The second night can sometimes be worse than the first night (sorry!) and the third night generally gets a little easier.

Once you've established this pattern and things are starting to settle in, you want to gradually withdraw the support you provide at the start. So every 4th night eliminate some aspect of how you are helping your child go to sleep. It may be the patting or the shushing. Choose what you are comfortable with and what seems right for your child. Make sure you do the same during the night when your child wakes. Keep up this new pattern for another four nights.

After four nights of the new, reduced pattern, eliminate one more element. You can pat or soothe but not during the final drift into sleep. Maybe this time you soothe from a bit of a distance, eliminating your close proximity to the crib. It doesn't matter what you eliminate and, of course, the things you can eliminate depends on what you included on the first night. Go at a speed you are comfortable with and try to pick up cues from your child.

Continue with this pattern of gradual reduction in sleep support and be sure to continue the reductions when your child wakes in the middle of the night. You just want to make sure you're making a step in the right direction every 4th night. Gradually transfer the responsibility for falling asleep to your child by gradually providing fewer supports.

This method works for children of all temperaments because it's build around your child's own particular likes and dislikes.

What About Nursing or Rocking To Sleep?

So… if The Michi Method lets you do what you like at the very beginning, can't you just nurse your child to sleep or rock him to sleep? Why not?

Certainly you can. I even know of one family that every night strapped the baby in a car seat and drove around until he fell asleep. There are lots of ways to make an infant sleepy. But methods like these don't solve the problem of teaching a child to settle on his own and get to sleep without props. And that's what you want to do.

On the other hand, if what you're doing is not a problem for you, then it's not a problem.

Strangely enough, natural and necessary though sleep is, a baby needs *to learn* how to get to sleep from a state of being awake. In order for that to happen, you will invest some time and patient effort in helping your child learn this essential skill. For many parents, though, the quiet time in a child's room at night is a lovely way to end their child's day.

Nursing your baby to sleep is almost unavoidable with a newborn. Rocking your baby to sleep or bouncing on an exercise ball is lovely in those first early months. But at some point - and if you're reading this book, you're at that point - you want your child to be able to fall asleep on his own.

Remember that if you're starting sleep training, you want to be consistent. You don't want to fall back on nursing-to-sleep or rocking-to-sleep. Give the method you've selected an honest try.

What About Nursing During The Night?
Keep in mind that if your child still needs feeding during the night that's part of your sleep routine. Set up a reasonable timing for these feeds, depending on

your child's feeding schedule during the day. If your child feeds every two hours during the day, then you will likely have a similar schedule during the night. The thing to keep in mind is that you want to keep to some sort of plan or schedule in the night. Nighttime is not the time when you want to feed your child whenever she wakes, just to quiet her. Stick to your plan.

To get your child back to sleep after a nighttime feed, just repeat the techniques you use for the go-to-bed routine. It's fine if your child falls asleep during a nighttime feed.

Once you have your child sleep-trained, you might think it's all downhill from there. Of course, it's not! There's plenty more to think about as your child grows towards toddlerhood. We'll think about those things in the next chapter.

Chapter Six
Sleep Issues In Toddlers

Let's imagine that you've finally got your baby sleeping through the night - however you define that - and things are going reasonably well. Is it smooth sailing from here?

Of course not! As you may have already discovered, things get interesting yet again when your baby becomes a toddler. Toddlers love being in charge! And being in charge of sleep is no exception. You may discover that your routines don't seem to fit anymore. It can seem like you're back to Square One in the sleep game. This can really make things a challenge and very frustrating.

Remember that you are the grown-up, you are in charge. Your toddler may not like the fact that you are, but remaining in charge is paramount to getting him past this stage quickly.

And the frustration? You can resolve your frustration at least a little bit by knowing more about what's going on now, as your child moves into the toddler years. We'll start with that.

Why Toddlers Are So Difficult

Babies in the nine-month to two-year range are "toddlers" - no longer helpless infants, these children are increasingly able to get around and to communicate their needs and wants. And they are increasingly self-aware. They have strong opinions about their own wishes and strong opinions about your totally inadequate efforts (to their mind) to satisfy their desires quickly enough.

Toddlers are a lot of fun. Finally, it seems, your hard work in those first few months are being rewarded by this charming, clever little person. Then you try to get her to sleep and the battles begin!

Physical Changes In The Toddler Years

One source of difficulty with toddlers is the rapid development of their bodies. This is something we parents sometimes forget to notice as a "problem." This development occurs most obviously in the mouth and the limbs.

> **Teething.** Teething makes children miserable. Not only do a child's gums hurt terribly, but teething also causes fever, congestion, irritability, and drool. Lots of drool. It should come as no surprise, then, that the teething toddler has difficulty going to sleep and may seem to need more naps, even as she refuses to take any naps at all.

> **Grasping.** Toddlers are increasingly able to grasp and hold objects deliberately. This is great. But it often means the toddler cannot give up his toys when it's bedtime. And if he takes his toys to bed, he may be kept awake

by them and by the inevitable dropping of toys that puts them out of reach.

Crawling, cruising and walking. The baby who has figured out how to get around seems driven to move, constantly. The crawler motors around her crib, seemingly unable to settle. The child who can pull to stand often first demonstrates this trick at the side of the crib. Putting him down to sleep is met with an almost instant stand, usually accompanied by loud protest.

Social-Emotional Growth In Toddlers

Physical growth triggers social or emotional issues that can interfere with children's sleep. Let's look at the most common of these.

Separation anxiety. It's as if the child who has learned to crawl suddenly realizes that if she can move away from you, you could just as easily move away from her! Separation anxiety - that clingy, whiney, mournful calling for closeness - happens just as a child starts to creep and can continue for several weeks. This is why starting sleep-training between 9 and 12 months is discouraged and why you'd do well to start childcare either ahead of this point or after it's passed. It's obvious that separation anxiety can interfere with your child's ability to settle for sleep - and why he seems to panic if he wakes in the night to find you're not there.

Need for autonomy. The toddler child wants to do everything himself. This includes turning off and on the light switches, picking out books to read, feeding himself, and walking on his own without holding anyone's hand. He has strong opinions and high expectations, for himself and for you. This is all lovely in its own way but it can certainly disrupt your daily routine or the evening wind-down.

Frustration. The child who is mobile and can put her thoughts into words feels she should rule the universe! These are amazing accomplishments but the toddler still can't do all the things she wants to do. Things still don't always go her way. Naturally, this is frustrating. The "Terrible Twos" arise out of the toddler's feelings of power and autonomy and her frustration at the limitations she still feels. These strong feelings spill over, often, at bedtime, when she's tired, when she wants to stay up longer, and when it seems like parents impose all their unnecessary rules.

The influence of temperament continues. Your child's temperament may be even more noticeable than before – in fact, the toddler years are the time when his temperament may finally come together clearly for you. And whether your child is Easy, Difficult, Slow-To-Warm-Up, or a combination, this preset point-of-view will affect everything that goes on. Keep your child's temperament in mind and remember to adjust your methods to *this* child, not to some other stereotypical child.

Toddler Sleep Regression

This is why you discover the sleep work you've done so far might suddenly appear to fall apart: regression. "Regression" means "going backwards" and that's exactly what this is. Just when you think your child is sleeping well, you hit a sleep regression and it seems that all your hard work is out of the window!

This is normal, okay? Don't worry, you've not lost all the hard work you've put into sleep training. And there are some things you can do to get back on track ASAP. Let me lay out when you can expect regression and after that talk about what to do about it.

9-month regression. There can be a little regression at four months (though you didn't start sleep training before that anyway, right?). But at nine months, a regression can hit and last up to six weeks – argh! Remember, there is a lot going on with your child at around 9 months old. She may be learning to crawl or pull to stand up. She is also entering the biggest phase of separation anxiety that she'll go through. This all makes leaving her to fall asleep independently a thing of the past.

12-month regression. Just when things were getting back to normal after the 9-month regression the 12-month regression hits! This regression isn't as long as the 9 month (thank goodness!).

109

Dear Rebecca -
Our recently completely-weaned 36 month-old boy is having trouble getting through the night. That's *36 months.*

He wants the light on and also he wakes at 3:30 every morning, thus waking the whole household. He is also thirsty and hungry at that time - perhaps a vestige of nursing?

He also frequently migrates into the hallway to sleep on the carpet. I'm sad for him. What can we do?

Dear Mum and Dad -
Could you put a sippy cup of water in or near his bed? You can work on getting him to take care of his desire for something to drink all on his own.

Also, if you haven't already, try a nightlight. Choose one which has more of an orange light, not a white, blue or LED light. The orange-y color will interfere less with sleep hormones.

Don't worry about him sleeping in the hall. If you find him on the floor, just take him back to his bed. It's very common for toddlers to want to sleep elsewhere!

18-month regression. Now things begin to get interesting! Your child will be more opinionated when it comes to going to sleep and may refuse to go down to sleep as easily as he used to. Remember what we said about autonomy?

24-month regression. Much the same as the 18-month regression. "You're not the boss of me!" is the slogan of the day.

What you need to do.
Obviously you want your child to get over the regression as quickly as possible. Except for the 9-month regression (more on that in a second), I think this is fairly easy to do. I suggest just going with the flow without introducing new habits. Don't try to start a whole new routine or imagine that the old routine "didn't work." Stick with it! Remember the importance of being consistent. If you continue with your usual routines and how you've dealt in the past with your child when she has trouble going down or wakes in the night, she will get over the regression quicker and you'll all be getting more sleep sooner.

And you *will* get less sleep during a regression. Be prepared for this and be prepared for being a little more tired during this time. Remember to share the burden with your partner!

Your child will need more help going to sleep during the 9-month regression. As your child is also most likely dealing with separation anxiety, getting back to normal can be more of a challenge.

I suggest giving your 9-month-old child the extra help, but without creating new habits. Sit next to your child whilst he falls asleep, but don't begin to rock him. Talk soothing, reassuring words to him, but don't give him a feed every time he wakes.

Daily routine is really important during this time. Having super consistent routines, for nap, nighttime and during the day, will make your child feel really secure and help him with the separation anxiety.

Things do get interesting when your baby becomes a toddler. Toddlers *love* being in charge! And being in charge of sleep is no exception. But a toddler in charge at bedtime doesn't fall asleep quickly or easily and will need your help many, many times a night. This can really make things a challenge.

Remember you are the grown up, you are in charge. Your toddler may not like the fact that you are, but remaining in charge is paramount to getting over these regressions quickly.

Other Toddler Sleep Issues

You thought regression was all of it? Oh, no! Here is a quick rundown of other sleep issues that can beset a toddler and his parents, along with a bit of advice for getting things back on track.

Getting To Sleep
"My child can't fall asleep on her own!"

If your child relies on something or someone to fall asleep and is unable to fall asleep independently, then now is the time to guide her in acquiring this key skill. Wait no longer to begin sleep training with real commitment. Check out the sleep training methods, choose a method which suits you, your family and your individual sleep needs. Then implement it carefully and consistently. Realize that the older your toddler is, the longer it might take to instill new habits, so be patient but don't give up!

"My child gets overtired and then can't fall asleep!"

I have this trouble too, don't you? Getting wound up late at night is certain to lead to tossing and turning for hours. It's the same for your child. The solution is obvious: try to ensure your child doesn't become overtired.

Watch your child for his tired signs. These may include rubbing his eyes, yawning, quieting down, becoming noisy and talkative, asking for his lovie, slowing down, or going glassy-eyed. (Your infant might not show any sleepy signs. He will as he gets older.) When your child shows you one of these signs, start your 10 to 15 minute naptime routine or your 35 to 45 minute nighttime routine. Don't wait!

If your child has had a particularly stimulating time before nap or bedtime you may want to introduce a 15 to 20 minute winding down *before* you start your child's routine. Doing this will help avoid the melt

Dear Rebecca -
Any tips for getting a 17 month old to learn to
fall asleep by himself? I have been nursing
him to sleep until about a month ago, and
unfortunately had to substitute with the bottle
now that we are weaned. I know I set myself
up for this, but now what?

Dear Mum –
Does he fall asleep whilst you're holding him
and he is drinking? If so, here's what to do:

Pop in the crib with the bottle and he can drink
the bottle himself. Initially you may need to
help him and hold the bottle for him. When he
is feeding himself, you can gradually reduce
down the amount of milk he is getting,
replacing it with water, if you like.

If you are worried about the amount of milk
he gets each day you could offer milk in a
sippy cup as part of your routine (instead of a
bottle, not in addition to a bottle) and then a
little soothe to sleep. When you get to
incorporated into your routine, you can
substitute the milk for water.

down that could occur if you try to move straight from running on fumes to heading off to bed.

Remember your daily routine. And remember that if your child is *temperamentally* more spirited, more driven, or more routine-dependent than other kids, you will need to take extra precautions against letting him get overtired.

"My child stands up the minute I put her down!"
This can be so frustrating! You had your child sleeping well, going down to sleep easily. Now that she's learnt to crawl or can stand in the crib, that's all she wants to do. When you put her down, she either jumps up or crawls around wailing like a lost puppy.

This can be an issue whenever your child reaches a milestone. She just can't not practice any new skills that she learns. Luckily this isn't something that lasts long, though it can happen over and over again for each new "trick."

If your child has learned to stand up but has yet to learn the skills to get back down, she can find herself stranded! So take time to practice getting down from a standing position. Play in the crib with your child at another time than nap or sleep time and practice letting go of the top rail, getting to sitting and then getting to lying down. Make this as fun as you can. And practice, practice, practice.

This is just a stage. If you are consistent with how you deal with going to sleep and with waking up and standing in the night, then it will solve itself in a day or two.

"My child throws up when I put him to bed!"
Oh, dear! Children who can make themselves throw up are usually over a year old. Your child may have initially vomited unintentionally, because of crying or illness. He quickly learned that when he vomits he gets taken out of bed, gets a lot of sympathy and concern, is given a bath and generally gets to stay up and have a good time for a while. Your clever little person has learned that throwing up can be used as a delaying tactic when it comes to going to bed.

You need to be firm to change this habit. As soon as you hear your child cough (kids usually cough before vomiting), say in a firm voice, "Henry, no!" Repeat as needed. If he does vomit, obviously you need to get him changed and cleaned up, but don't give him a bath and don't give him any sympathy. In fact, don't say anything at all. Be quick (it helps if your partner pitches in, with one of you cleaning up the bed and the other cleaning up the child). Do not go through the bedtime routine again, just get your child straight back to bed with as much speed and as little attention paid as possible.

Have spare PJs, cleaning supplies, and so on ready before getting your child down. This makes for an easier and quicker cleanup.

If you don't think your child is making himself throw up, if he's not coughing but vomits as soon as he lies down, then get him checked out by a doctor. You want to rule out any medical reason such as reflux for the vomiting.

Waking In The Middle Of The Night
"My child cries when she loses her pacifier!"
How you handle this depends on your child's age. If you just want to get your child out of the pacifier habit, then you'll need to work on that, probably starting during the daytime. It's easier to get your child away from the pacifier if you do it before your child is six months old, before the habit is fully entrenched, or after three years old, when you're able to reason with your child. If your child is somewhere between six months and three years and if you just want to solve the problem of waking up to search for a lost pacifier, then there are a few things you can do.

- Put plenty - at least six - pacifiers in the bed or crib.
- Teach your child how to put the pacifier into her own mouth.
- Spend some time playing with your child in the crib or bed, hiding pacifiers and finding them again.

Take time during the day to teach your child how to find her pacifier and reinsert it, all on her own. Put her love of autonomy to work for you!

Just remember: never, ever tie a pacifier to the bars of the crib or to your child.

"My child wakes at the same time each night!"
This is a habitual waking. One great way to stop this habit is by waking your child just a bit before he usually wakes. I know this sounds crazy: waking you child up from a sound sleep. But give it a try. If your child wakes every night at 3:15 AM, set your alarm for

117

Dear Rebecca -
Our daughter is 15 months old and doesn't even come close to sleeping thru the night. She wants to nurse every 3 hours and wakes up an hour after she falls asleep. She only nurses at night as we have weaned day feedings. If my husband tries to comfort her she screams and cries to the point of throwing up and gagging. If I won't let her nurse, she has the same reaction to me. We co-sleep by the way. Will she eventually grow out of it? Thanks for your help!

Dear Mum -
I think making some changes now would be a good idea. Your daughter is in control of bedtimes and the night wakings. At the moment she has no desire to change the way things are going, she gets what she wants and when she wants it. If she doesn't she knows what she needs to do to get it.

You need to take back control. If you no longer want to nurse through the night, stop. Be with her when she's mad and frustrated. Rocking, walking with her, singing, etc., will all help her settle. Once she realizes you are not going to give in, she will not get so mad and the crying will stop.

If nursing has been getting her to sleep you may want to have a look at some sleep training techniques. Good luck!

3 AM. Go to your child and rouse him from a deep sleep. Just rub his back, pat his tummy gently, call his name, and then let them go back into a deep sleep. Don't wake your child up fully. Rouse him just enough to break the cycle of waking. Do this for three nights and then see if your child sleeps through.

"My child wakes during the night and is ready to party!"

If your child is awake for long periods at night, playing and keeping you awake, then the chances are she is in charge during the night. You need to get back in charge. Let your child know that from bedtime until morning time she needs to remain in her bed. If she wakes during the night, be in control. Put her back to bed, don't make eye contact, don't talk about anything, just be Robot Mom, putting her back down with no nonsense allowed. Your child will soon learn that she must stay in bed and that her demands are fruitless. Do expect a few rough nights. Your child will only change this habit if you remain super consistent. Don't give in!

Feeding In The Night
"My toddler wants to nurse all night long!"

Probably your child is nursing throughout the night because he hasn't yet learned the skills to get himself to sleep on his own. Remember that your child doesn't need food during the night. Nursing at night is a habit you can break.

Throughout the night we all go through sleep cycles. We go into a deep sleep and come into a lighter sleep.

As adults we may come into a light sleep, roll over and go back to sleep. We barely wake up. We have learned how to get ourselves back to sleep. If your child doesn't have the skills to fall asleep independently, if instead he gets nursed, rocked, soothed, and so on, then he will rely on that to get himself back to sleep.

Time to teach your child the skills he needs. Read through the sleep training techniques and choose one which suits you and your family.

"My toddler demands a bottle during the night!"
If your toddler is used to drinking large quantities of milk during the night, the chances are she's going to be hungry during the night if you go cold turkey and completely stop the bottle. There are a few ways you can reduce the night feedings and prepare for sleep training if needed.

Reduce the amount of milk offered during the feed by one ounce every second night. For a quicker reduction you can replace one or two ounces each night with water. Once you've got your child down to having only water you can leave a sippy cup of water next to the bed. Quite often when watering down milk, children don't want to have any more when you get to about 50-50.

If your child is still waking after reducing the milk, treat this like waking at the same time each night..

Sleep And Illness
"My child is teething or sick and can't sleep!"
Illness can always mess up your child's sleep. If your child suddenly wakes up in the night when this is not her pattern, if she was strangely fussy during the day and you are unable to get her settle, then I would presume something is causing her discomfort. Check her diaper, check her temperature, see if she seems bothered by something you can identify. Could your child be teething? Some teething signs are red cheeks, drooling excessively, putting hands into her mouth, pulling on her ears, chewing on toys, and so on.

Keep medications and a thermometer and so on handy but stored safely. Know what your plan of action is. Devise your plan during the day. Are you going to soothe first and then get medication? If you're going to get medication write down what you give and at what time. In a sleep deprived state you don't want to give an accidental overdose. Wait at least 20 minutes after giving medication before you try to get her back to sleep.

Be prepared to help your child more during the night if she's suffering from an illness or teething. This is no fun for anyone!

"My child is over an illness or a bout of teething, but is still waking during the night!"
Your child's sleep patterns were naturally disrupted during the time he was sick. But now that he's feeling better, you need to get him back on track.

If you initially used one of the sleep training techniques to teach your child to fall asleep independently, just use the same one now. It won't take as long as it initially did - maybe just a night or two. It depends on how long your child was unwell or teething. The longer the disruption, the longer it takes to get back on track.

If you didn't use one of the sleep training techniques before, now is the time to choose one. As your child was sleeping well before the teething or illness it shouldn't take long to get back to normal.

I know that you're tired after being at the 24-hour beck and call of an unwell child but the longer you put off getting him back on schedule, the harder it will be to get back to a good night's sleep for everyone.

Chapter Seven
Sleep Issues In Preschoolers

Now that your child is a preschooler – which I'm going to count as being between ages three and five, though obviously "it depends" – you may be surprised to find that there still are sleep issues. (!!!!) Let's talk about the ones you're most likely to encounter. Before we do, though, we'll find out more about what's going on for youngsters this age.

The Preschool Mentality

Your preschool child may be so verbal and so clever that you could be deceived into believing she thinks just like you do. You may expect that you can get her to do what you want just by explaining things – even just by explaining things *only once*.

But your preschooler and you are still not quite on the same page in many ways. Here are some of the reasons why.

Uneven memory
Your child's brain at this age is still developing its ability to remember episodes – things that happened and their consequences. This ability just got going at about age three. (How old were you at your earliest memory? Chances are you were three.) This means that three-year-olds can't remember what happened "the last time you pulled that stunt," and even four-year-olds can be fuzzy. Kids this age won't remember

Dear Rebecca -
My son is 4, and I just learned he has sensory integration disorder. He does not process things as well as he should, or over processes them. He is absolutely 100% terrified to the point of a panic attack to sleep on his own. We tried it for a while and he did ok, but maybe for a few months we had success (I can't tell you what changed). Now he has to have someone lie with him to go to bed. If he is alone, he does have a full blown panic attack. (his SID really makes his emotions extra heightened and fear grows more than it should). How can we teach him to sleep on his own?

Dear Mum -
I would make sure that your bedtime routine is very, very consistent. Make sure you are doing the same things in the same place in the same order, every night.

You want to slowly work on getting yourself out of the room whilst he falls asleep. Firstly work on sitting on the bed not lying, then next to the bed, and then slowly making your way towards the door. Make a change every 4th night. Don't rush it, but don't go too slow either.

Your Physical Therapist may have some suggestions for calming and relaxing before bed. Good luck.

at bedtime what you said in the morning, much less what you said yesterday or the day before.

Limited experience

Preschoolers talk a good game and they can be amazingly perceptive. But they don't have much experience, they are not able to take another person's point-of-view very well, and they are unclear about the consequences of their actions. They have an imperfect notion of time, in fact, they pretty much live in the present, with only fuzzy understanding of the past and the future. They have limited vocabularies and limited grasp of concepts. Too much talk just goes over their heads.

Increasing powers of imagination

What preschoolers lack in real life experience they make up for in fantasy. It's all the same to kids this age – the line between fact and fiction is very blurry. This means that preschoolers can feel vulnerable to all sorts of imagined dangers – everything from monsters under the bed to robbers - and these can keep them up at night.

Sensitive to shame but also demanding of respect

Shame and embarrassment are what psychologists call "self-conscious emotions." They require the development of self-awareness and an understanding of the difference between our own feelings and the judgments of someone else. These are new abilities of the preschool years and new emotions. Preschoolers can feel acutely embarrassed by not measuring up to adult standards and also can feel deeply stung by insensitive comments. At this time when parents are ready for their children to act "grown-up," it's easy to say the wrong thing.

Still ruled by temperament and preset ways of interacting

Your child will never outgrow his temperament. The highly reactive infant became a high-strung toddler and will grow into a drama-queen preschooler. The laid-back baby is still laid-back. The reserved and careful child will always be reserved and careful. These are the charms your child brings to your family and they're all good. Don't wish any of it away. More than ever, help your child to manage her feelings and feel comfortable out and about but don't try to change who she is.

All right. Given all that, what are the issues that will come up at bedtime and what can you do about them? We'll talk here about sleeping in a new bed, sleep and toilet training, and managing dreams and nightmares. In later chapters we'll talk about naps and issues related to family disruptions, like the arrival of a new baby.

New Places To Sleep

One of the big changes that happens sometime during the late-toddler and early preschool years is the move to some sort of "big bed." What you need to do to help this transition happen smoothly depends in part of your child's starting point and the situation you're trying to move her to.

Quitting Co-Sleeping

If you've continued co-sleeping into your child's toddler or preschool years, then there's more to quitting than just deciding one day to move him into his own bed. Of course, your child will have been napping in his own bed all along. But sleeping there in the night may seem new and strange. Expect a bit of upset.

Talk with your child during the day about sleeping in his own bed at bedtime. Ask your child what he wants to take with him to sleep in his bed in the night. Then do all the evening routine activities that you can (getting on jammies, reading a story, and so on) in his own room. Choose a sleep-training technique to use as a fallback so you know what you will do if he cries and carries on.

Then stick with it. Do not give in or let him come into your bed in the middle of the night. If you waffle it will be even harder to make this transition later.

Make sure you're scheduling plenty of snuggle time with your child throughout the day, since this is the chief benefit of co-sleeping that will be lacking when he's sleeping on his own. Let him know you're pleased and proud of him and that you still love to cuddle!

Moving Out Of The Crib

Is your child ready to move out of the crib into her very own, big kid bed? Here are some things to keep in mind:

First, your child should be at least 12 months old before moving out of her crib. You want your child to be old enough to be able to stay in the bed, instead of rolling out of it. If your child is younger or if your main motivation is that she can climb out of the crib anyway, check to see if the crib too small. You may be able to delay a move to a big bed by lowering the crib mattress.

But, second, I do think the move is easier the younger your child is but moving your child's bed is most challenging for two-year-olds. So make changes to sleeping arrangements either before two or after three. Toddlers - especially spirited ones and children who are slow-to-warm-up -can get really attached to things, which may make the move a tough one if you let habits get too entrenched.

Once you've decided that this is indeed the time to move from a crib to a big bed, then it helps if you can do this in a stepwise fashion. If your child's crib has been in your bedroom but the new toddler bed is in the child's own room down the hall, then it works best to make one change at a time: move the crib into the new room first, then once that transition has been made, switch the crib out for a big bed. Make this sort of change early in the day, so your child has a chance to sleep in his crib the new location for his nap and has a chance to play in the new room during the day before sleeping there in the night.

If your child's crib is already in a room of his own, then keeping the crib in that room and adding the big bed, so the child can use the crib sometimes and try out the big bed at other times, is a good strategy for easing in the new sleeping arrangement. Your child can use the big bed for naps, for example, and retain the crib for nighttime for a little while.

But many families have a convertible crib – one that becomes a twin-size bed by removing the crib sides. For these families, there is no option to have both the crib and a new big bed available. If this is your situation, then involve your child in the process of removing the crib side and trying out the new toddler bed. Do this early in the day and spend some time playing in and around the converted bed so the strangeness can wear off a bit by bedtime.

Do expect your child to get out of bed. She now will have the freedom to do that if she wishes and I'm sure she will wish it. When she does, simply take her straight back to bed. Don't engage in conversation. Just say, "It's nap time' or 'It's night time" and "It's time to stay in bed" and repeat as needed. Children might get out of their beds many, many times at first. It can take two or three days for them to remain in bed once you've tucked them in.

If getting out of bed continues to be a problem, you can stay outside the room, lying in wait. As soon as you see hear him get out of bed, say in a stern voice, "Stay in bed!" If he continues to get out of bed go into his room and take him back to bed without any eye contact or comment.

Also, expect your child to fall out of bed. Your child will quickly learn the limits of the bed's surface and

Dear Rebecca -
I am working on getting 22 month old Oliver through a sleep regression brought on by illness and travel. He doesn't go down easily and is up every hour after his 4 hour bout of deep sleep at the beginning of the night. The other night he jumped out of his crib.

I know it's time to take the side off the crib for safety reasons. Do I deal with the sleep issues first and camp out in his room till he sleeps through the night again, or bite the bullet and move him to the toddler bed and deal with the waking issues all at one time? By the way, he was thrilled to have hopped the crib. He danced into our room with a big grin!

Dear Dad -
Oh no, jumping out of the crib?!

It depends how brave you are! If you're really brave, just go for it. It will be initially a little harder, but you'll have it all done quicker. The night waking may not be as bad when moved into the bed.

If instead you want to stop him jumping out of the crib, wait outside of the room with the door open a tiny bit. When you see Oliver starting to climb out, tell him, in a firm voice, to stay in his bed. If he continues, take him back and pop him back in.

Have you seen the crib tents? Some people love these.

will be able to stay on it pretty reliably even while sound asleep. But before this learning takes hold, children might fall out. There are removable bed guards you can slide under the mattress but this is not the best method for teaching a child how to stay on the bed. Children can get trapped between the mattress and the bed guard. Another method is to simply put pillows or couch cushions on the floor beside the bed so when your child rolls out she will land on a softer surface.

Keep in mind that your small child should never sleep in an upper bunk bed or in any bed that is elevated off the floor by more than 24" or so.

Remember to make sure that your child's room is safe for them. It's a good idea to keep tempting toys out of the way for a little while, lock the closet door and even turn the dresser around so a child can't open the drawers. Make sure there are no new climbing opportunities and that there are no cords anywhere a child on her own could get tangled up in. Make certain any windows are securely shut.

Sleep and Toileting

About the time you move your child into a bed of his own, with the freedom to get up on his own, you will also be working on toilet training. Most children still need a diaper during the night until about age three or even four. But until a child is able to control his urine for the entire night, you may encounter an issue or two.

The first issue is that your child may get up repeatedly to use the potty. This can be incredibly frustrating, even as it signals how well your child is doing on the toilet-training. Unfortunately there isn't much we can do in this situation. Your child will start producing the hormone called antidiuretic ADH sometime during the toddler or preschool period. This hormone reduces the amount of urine produced whilst asleep. Until this happens your child may wake during the night needing to use the bathroom.

You can wake your child and take him to the bathroom before you go to bed. If you would like your child to take himself to the bathroom make sure he understands what to do. Decide if you want him to use the toilet in the bathroom or use a potty in his own room. Understand that whatever you choose, you will still need to monitor the situation to avoid unnecessary anxiety and frustration for the child – feelings that can set back the whole toilet training program – and to avoid mess.

Toilet-training at night works the best when you are okay with diapers until it's obvious – by repeated dry diapers in the morning – that your child is able to last until morning.

Wetting the Bed

Bedwetting is not considered a problem unless is lasts past age five. This means it's not a signal of any underlying problem until a child is into elementary school, though this doesn't mean it's not a challenge for you and for your child. Generally speaking, boys have more difficulty with bedwetting than girls do.

If you or your partner wet the bed at night as a child, your child is more likely to. There is a strong genetic component to this. In any case, wetting the bed is not something your child does on purpose and it's not something that can be fixed by using threats, punishments, or even bribery. Believe me, your child doesn't like this either and would stop it if he could.

For most kids, solving bedwetting is simply a matter of maturation. Your child just needs more growing up in this area than the average kid. So find no-fault ways of managing the problem: use pajama pants – absorbent underwear designed just for this purpose and just for these older children. Keep fresh bedding on hand, use a mattress and pillow protector, and just clean up as necessary. Limit liquids in the hour before bed and consider getting your child up in the night for a bathroom break. The more sympathetic and supportive you can be the easier it will be for your child to learn to hold her urine. Anxiety and shame are counter-productive and may add to the problem, not solve it.

If bed wetting lasts long enough to be a concern, and especially if your child is concerned and unhappy, talk to your pediatrician. There are medications that can help and that may be just the boost your child needs to master this ability.

Dear Rebecca -
We finally merged our 2 boys (3½ and 8) into the same room, moving the younger out of our bedroom. It's going better than expected, but I have to sit in there till they fall asleep, which involves repeating that it's time for bed many times. And multiple bathroom trips before falling asleep even though I have started limiting fluids after 7 pm.

Usually I can't get them to sleep before 9 pm, and the younger one usually wakes between 6 and 7 am. He seems to still need a nap so I have been aiming for an early nap of about an hour. If I let him nap longer then he can't get to sleep at night, but if I keep him up entirely he is out of control in the afternoon. Ideas??

Dear Mum -
I would try limiting the nap to 45 minutes. You may need to give it a week before you see any changes.

You'll want to have a nice calm and quiet bedtime routine. Around 30 minutes should be fine. Make it very consistent. No TV or rough and tumble play. Carry on limiting fluids.

I wouldn't get into bed with your son. Sit with him whilst he falls back asleep. You don't want to end up spending the whole night in bed with him. Good luck!

The New Evening Routine

Your old bedtime routine won't work so well, now that your child is older, as it worked when she was an infant or toddler. But the evening routine is still important. Your child still needs help in winding down and getting mentally and physiologically ready for sleep. Here are some tips.

Bedtime snack

Some foods can actually help your child sleep! These are foods high in the amino acid tryptophan. Tryptophan has a calming effect on the brain making it easier to fall and stay asleep. The body converts the amino acid into serotonin and melatonin.

In general, foods which will help a person fall asleep have small amounts of protein and are high in complex carbohydrates. Calcium also helps with the absorption of tryptophan and melatonin production. So here are some examples of foods that are high in the right stuff:

- Whole grain cereal with milk
- A bowl of oatmeal with milk
- Peanut butter sandwich on whole wheat bread with a glass of milk
- A turkey sandwich on whole wheat bread with a glass of milk
- Oatmeal raisin cookies and milk
- An apple with cheese
- Yoghurt with granola
- A banana and a handful of almonds
- A date or bran muffin with a glass of milk

At the same time, there are definitely foods to avoid. Beverages and foods that contain caffeine, like chocolate, cocoa, and sodas, are obviously poor choices for bedtime snacks. Simple carbohydrates in sweets may also interfere with settling down. If your child is sensitive to food dyes you will want to avoid those as well.

Elements of the New Routine

Preschoolers can do more than toddlers and that can lead to doing too much in the time after dinner. It is important to limit overstimulation of all sorts, including roughhousing, homework and exciting or disturbing television programs. Studies have shown that screen time in the evening – computer play, playing with handhelds, video games and even TV – all interfere with melatonin production. As you know, melatonin is the hormone responsible for making us feel sleepy – it's not something you want to interfere with for your child. So while you are limiting overstimulation, limit screen time too.

What's left? Reading aloud together. Playing board games that are not stressful. Drawing, painting, playing with building sets and toys figures. Going for a walk around the neighborhood in the gathering dusk. The calmer, quieter and slower you can make your preschooler's evening, the more ready he will be for sleep.

Once your child is in bed, be sure to keep things low-key. Many children like to have a night light on but keep in mind that any light interferes with melatonin.

Studies have shown that the darker the room, the sounder the sleep. So do not assume your child "needs" a night light and if she thinks this is truly a necessity, opt for the dimmest light possible.

Children should not have the television or computer on in their room or watch a DVD player. If you like, you may permit your child to take books to bed and it's okay to play quiet music of the sort that doesn't make a child want to dance along. Remember that children need to learn how to settle themselves for sleep. Do nothing that interferes with this work.

Chapter Eight
Dreams And Other Disturbances

Preschool children may start to report having dreams. Worse, they may be awakened by scary dreams, disrupting your sleep and maybe making you wonder what's going on. Let's talk in this chapter about dreams, scary dreams, night terrors, and sleepwalking.

Dreams

Recall what we said at the very beginning about sleep cycles. All sleep is not the same, but changes throughout the night, rising and falling into deeper and lighter levels in a regular pattern. Dreams happen during Rapid Eye Movement sleep. In REM sleep, the body is unable to move (which keeps us from acting out our dreams). The brain is as active during REM sleep as it is when the dreamer is wide awake.

And this last is a clue about the importance of REM sleep: the brain is active, solidifying memories and filing away what was learned during the day. The brain needs this period of bodily and mental inactivity so the way is cleared for its own work. People who do not get adequate amounts of REM sleep – including those who don't get enough uninterrupted sleep to get to the REM point of the sleep cycle and also including those who take sleep aids, which short-circuit the sleep cycle pattern – have trouble remembering things and struggle to use the information they thought they had learned. If you have missed getting enough REM sleep because of several nights of interrupted sleep, you likely will have many more dreams on the night when you finally get your full eight hours. You've got to catch up!

So dreams are important because REM sleep is important. Even if you don't remember your dreams, you *are* dreaming, about 25% of the time in any one night. Younger children have more REM sleep than adults do. Premature infants may be in REM sleep up to 80% of their sleep time. Long before your preschooler reports having a dream, your child has been dreaming, every night (and maybe even during long naps).

Dreams At Different Ages
We have no idea what babies dream of. Dream researchers typically wake up a sleeper when her eyes begin to twitch during Rapid Eye Movement sleep and ask her what she was thinking about. So knowledge about dream content depends on being able to understand this question and on being able to give an answer.

Toddlers and preschoolers report dreaming about things, without any story attached to them. So they dream about a dog, about a bird, about a boat. Of course the dog might be a *scary* dog and the bird might be a *giant* bird and the boat might be broken and disturbing. Children aged four or five can describe a dream but they're not sure what was going on. The line between fact and fiction is still fuzzy at this age and children may actually think the dream is in the room with them, not in their heads.

Older children, from about age six or so, include themselves in their dreams and maybe familiar situations and people. Dreams start to have a story line and they can wake kids up with a scary feeling. Because these children understand about thinking thoughts, they realize that dreams are not physically real. But that doesn't make scary dreams less frightening.

Dreams that tell a story really get going in the preteen years. These dreams seem to mean something and children ages 10 and up report enjoying some of these dreams and being terrified by others of them. Dreams start to seem to "mean something."

Bad Dreams
Bad dreams are no fun. They will probably disturb your sleep even more than they disturb your child's sleep, since once you get him fully awake, get him a sip of water, and soothe him a bit, he will go right back to sleep. You, on the other hand, will be fully awake.

Scary dreams seem to be linked to developmental changes. As children get ready for a growth spurt or for some cognitive leap, bad dreams surface. It's as if the brain, busy with so much to do, linking up new ideas and making neural connections in response to sudden developmental shifts, lashes out with dreams that growl and terrify. This, at least, is a comforting thought, as you sympathize with your child in the middle of the night: that bad dreams mean progress and growth.

Dear Rebecca –
My almost 4 year-old is having nightmares. They've increased dramatically in frequency (many wakeups each night). The dreams occur early in the night, before deep sleep, and once they start she wakes frequently crying and calling out. When we go to her she settles down and goes back to sleep instantly, but wakes again 20 min later crying again.

She is also complaining about leg pains. She's an anxiety-prone kid and had 2 night terrors one week about 1 ½ years ago. I explained dreams on your suggestion (she was incredulous!), we made a homemade dream catcher, we've talked about her dream content, I've tried leg cramp prevention (water, potassium, and a homeopathic). Other ideas to calm her anxiety?

Dear Mum –
The leg pains may be growing pains (there really are such things!). I don't think there's a connection to her dreams.

Have there been any changes in her life or your family that could be upsetting her?

You might try the Wake-to-Sleep method, rousing her just before a "scheduled" dream. Do this every night for a week or so and see if you can break the pattern. I also wouldn't discuss dream content anymore unless she brings it up. That may actually inspire dreams.

Bad dreams can also be triggered by scary or disturbing media. Restricting what your child watches on television can help reduce the number of bad dreams. This includes not only stories and movies but also disturbing news accounts. Older preschoolers and elementary-school children are particularly sensitive to reports of wars, kidnappings and murders and can carry worry about their safety to bed with them.

Disturbing dreams can also be triggered by stress. If your child is troubled by dreams over more than a night or two, stop and think if there is something going on, at home or at school, that might be upsetting your child. See if you can smooth things over, dialing down the level of upset in her environment so she can sleep better at night.

Resist the temptation to analyze your child's dreams or to make a bigger deal about them than is necessary. Being sympathetic but unconcerned is the way to go. Dreams *are* normal, even if they are a new thing for your child.

Night Terrors

At first glance, a night terror seems like just another bad dream. Your child is crying – no, *screaming* – and it's the middle of the night. But that's where the resemblance stops. Unlike a bad dream, you cannot stop a night terror. The child seems awake but is not.

Dear Rebecca –
I was a sleepwalker as a child and I'm worried that my daughter is becoming a sleepwalker too. Twice in the last couple weeks I've heard her wandering around in the middle of the night. I get up and tuck her back in but I wonder what will happen if some night I don't hear her. Do you have any advice for me? (By the way, she's four.)

Dear Mum –
See if she's getting up at the same time each night. If so, you might try the Wake-to-Sleep method to bring her to a lighter sleep level for a few minutes just before a sleepwalking episode happens. This should disrupt the pattern. Do it for a few nights in a row.

Make sure, also, that she's not needing to use the toilet. This could be waking her enough to cause her to walk around but not enough to be aware of what she's doing.

Keeping a log might help you figure out if there is a trigger and will help you know if you need to guard against her wandering outside or something like that.

Most children outgrow this. It could help you to talk with your own parents and see if they can add some information.

Good luck with this!

He cannot hear you. You cannot soothe him. No, night terrors are not dreams. But they *are* terrifying.

A night terror doesn't happen in REM sleep. Instead it occurs in the deepest levels of sleep, when your child is absolutely unconscious but also able to move around. You cannot reach him in this sleep level and you are unlikely to be successful in waking him up. Really the only thing you can do is let the night terror run its course – it will be over in 5 or 10 minutes – and then tuck him back in and go back to bed yourself.

Night terrors tend to happen in three- and four-year-olds. They sometimes seem linked to some sort of daytime anxiety, including a move to a new home, the arrival of a new baby, or some other upset. Children who are overtired for any reason may also experience a night terror.

However, you can use the Wake To Sleep technique. Usually a night terror happens at the same time every night, often around 11:30 pm or midnight. So instead of waiting anxiously for the night terror to happen, wake your child about 15 minutes ahead of a "scheduled" episode. Take your child to the bathroom or get her a sip of water. Get her fully waked up and talking to you, then tuck her back in. If you can break the cycle for a day or two it likely will be broken for good.

Sleepwalking

Sleepwalking is another disturbance that happens in the deepest levels of sleep. You will not be successful in waking the sleepwalker and even though she appears to be awake, and can talk and walk (obviously), she is not really conscious. Your role is to guide her safely back to bed.

Sleepwalking has an hereditary component. If you or the child's other parent was (or is) a sleepwalker, then that may be the cause of your child's sleepwalking. If this is the case, then sleepwalking may last into the child's elementary school years and even into adulthood. You might consult your pediatrician for a recommendation of a sleep clinic if sleepwalking runs in the family and presents more than the usual level of challenge for you.

Sleepwalking is not dangerous unless the child does unsafe things while walking around unconscious. Children who go outside while asleep are clearly in danger. Do not, of course, tie a child into bed or make it so the child cannot escape his room in an emergency. But do make certain that your child cannot fall down the stairs or go out the front door.

Sleepwalking may be triggered by daytime stress or by developmental changes. Do what you can to dial down the stress during the day and to make certain the evening routine is calming. But unless you suspect sleepwalking is hereditary, you can be pretty confident it will disappear on its own.

Sleep Disturbances and Temperament

As you might guess, children with a Difficult temperament are more likely to report bad dreams than are children who have an Easy temperament. Anxious children – who may be Slow-To-Warm-Up – also have a slightly higher rate of bad dreams than do Easy children.

Night terrors also are more likely in Difficult children, as is sleepwalking.

The Difficult child, who is more "on" than other children, may need more help to settle down before bed. He may need you to monitor even more closely the sorts of media and other "inputs" he gets during the day, to keep these from disturbing his sleep. The Slow-To-Warm-Up child, who is more tightly wound than most and more prone to anxiety generally, also may need a calmer atmosphere and more support during the day than you might think necessary.

Studies have shown the link between temperament and bad dreams but also a link between supportive parenting and fewer bad dreams. Be sure to support your child, no matter what her temperament, and understand that dreams – the good ones and the bad ones – are a normal part of life.

Dear Rebecca –
My son Henry has decided there are monsters that live in his room that come out at night. The minute the lights are out, he starts to panic. We've tried using a nightlight, letting him sleep with a ray gun (it's a toy, of course), and talking him through it. He's all fine and logical until he goes to bed. Help!

Dear Dad –
You don't say how old Henry is, but I'm assuming he's three or older. If that's right, have a talk with him about this problem sometime during the day. Describe what the problem is (he is upset, the family is frustrated, and so on) and ask him what he thinks the solution might be.

Accept any reasonable suggestions, so if he says he wants to sleep with the overhead light on, fine. But if he says he wants to sleep in your room, that's not fine – it's not reasonable. Before bed, remind him of the plan and then support him in putting the plan in play if he feels anxious after bed. You want to help him feel empowered and capable. You might find stickers or tokens help.

This sort of thing will probably go away on its own eventually. But also make certain he's not being overstimulated by scary stuff during the day. Best wishes!

Chapter Nine
Naps

Is there anything more lovely than a nap? I don't think so! And yet, children - who are invited to take naps on a regular basis - soon (too soon!) decide to give them up. What are the tricks for managing naps?

Napping By Age

Let's be honest: newborns never sleep, they *nap*. They nap for an hour or two round the clock, daytime and nighttime. After several weeks or a few months of this, they start to nap longer at night, to the point that we can call this sleeping, and they nap about three times during the day. Unless they are sick, infants fall asleep anywhere, anytime and there is not much need to be concerned about scheduling a nap. Naps just happen.

By three months of age or so, babies have fallen into a more regular pattern of three naps a day. The three naps consolidate into two somewhere around nine months and then dwindle to just a single afternoon nap before 18 months or thereabouts. This wonderful, final nap hangs around until your child is three, or four, or even five years old. Parents and caregivers cherish this break in the action every afternoon. Preschoolers, sooner or later, resist.

Naps fill in a key portion of a child's daily sleep requirement. Babies need a minimum of 14 hours (and as many as 18 hours) of sleep in every 24 and certainly they are not doing all this sleeping at night! Three-year-olds need 12 to 14 hours of sleep and fours and fives need 11 or 12. So as the need for sleep reduces, the need for naps reduces too. The trick for moms and dads is to manage the nap reduction so children don't get overtired during the day and also are not too well-rested for sleep at night.

Naps And Your Schedule

A common problem with naptime management is the feeling that one must arrange daily activities so a child can be home napping at the proper time each day. This is all very well when an infant is tiny and you need your naps too. In addition, since babies nap perfectly well in a car seat or in a baby carrier, you can run errands while your very small child naps wherever he is without much difficulty.

Your ability to maintain this sort of casual, nap-on-the-fly flexibility into the toddler period depends in large part on your child's temperament. Naturally, Easy children are the most portable, the most able to catnap in the car, and the least likely to melt down if a nap isn't provided at the proper time and place.

The Slow-To-Warm-Up child may have more difficulty. She may need her bed, her lovey, and her routine and she may whine and fuss if she can't get these as needed. If you know you will be out and about during naptime, plan ahead to take her comfort objects along, including a pacifier if she uses one.

150

The Difficult child might be an eager goer, right up to the point when he completely falls apart. An overtired Difficult child is even more challenging than usual and it's unfair, really, to put your little person in this spot. Once overtired, your Difficult child may struggle more than other children to fall asleep at all, for a nap or even later at bedtime. It's in the best interests of everyone to accommodate your Difficult child by trying to maintain a naptime routine as precisely as you can.

The Naptime Routine

We talked quite a bit about naptime routines in Chapter Four. The bottom line is that having a routine that leads up to a nap is a good idea. It gets the child in the right frame of mind for sleep, both psychologically and physically. Remember that the sleep hormone melatonin is your friend and the way to trigger the on-time release of that is to build in patterns that signal the body that it's time for a nap.

It's a good idea to incorporate into your regular at-home nap routine rituals that can be duplicated just about anywhere. If you encourage your child to have a comfort object, and if you always read the same book and sing the same gentle songs ahead of a nap, then these are things you can take along on a day you know will keep you away from home at naptime. You can bring along the book and blankie on a long day of shopping, on a trip to Grandma's house, and anywhere else you may find yourself.

Dear Rebecca -
My five month old is a fairly good night time sleeper, but naps during the day are another story. She is not really on a schedule because her naps are all over the place. Mainly they are 45 minute cat naps and she needs four or more of these throughout the day or she is miserable.

I have tried all the tricks, longer awake time, shorter awake time, longer soothing time, white noise, patting her as she wakes to try and get her back to sleep, etc. Once in a while she will take a long morning nap but this is not her normal behavior.

Any suggestions or words of wisdom?

Dear Mum -
Try sticking to one routine for a week or more. You won't see instant changes when it comes to sleep unfortunately. Around two hours awake should be fine for her age. Make sure she is nice and relaxed for a little while before you begin to get her ready for a nap.

How does she get to sleep? It may be a good idea to teach her how to fall asleep independently. That way she will be able to get herself back into a deep sleep when she begins to wake too soon.

Obviously, napping away from home is not so good as napping in one's own bed. If you find that a nap was missed, do what you can to arrange things so your child can fall asleep at night pretty much on schedule. The key is to also avoid letting your child get overtired as you await nightfall on a day when the nap was missed.

No More Naps!

At about age three, most children will give up their nap. Some kids still nap into the four-year-old year and that's fine. But don't be too quick to believe your two-year-old has outgrown his nap. Children this age often go through a phase where they are awake all afternoon, seemingly doing fine. But they can't sustain this pace more than a few days. Twos need a lot of sleep, remember, and that pretty much has to include at least one nap during the day.

So let's assume your child is three or four and he's ready to give up his nap. He does well after lunch and maybe far into the afternoon. If you want him to carry on till bedtime without a nap, then mind that he doesn't fall asleep on his own just before dinnertime. If he does that, the whole evening schedule will be thrown off. Try offering a late-afternoon snack to help him power through or try moving bedtime to a bit earlier.

Giving up the nap may be uneven for the first few weeks. Some days your child will need a nap just as she did months ago. Some days she'll be fine without

153

one. You do need to stay flexible and watch to see what your child needs each day so she can get sleep if it's necessary. This transition period can be a bit tricky but it won't last long.

Consider switching out naptime for "quiet time" each day. Especially if you are home with your child – maybe also with a younger sibling – you all need a break in the afternoon to reset the day. You can do this with a nap that is not a nap: set a timer for 30 minutes or so and both of you take a quiet break to look at books, read, or just play quietly. Your child can spend this time in her room, even in her bed, but without any expectation for sleeping. This is a good technique, too, when your child is trying to give up her nap but sometimes still needs one.

Some signs your child is ready to drop his nap include
- Trouble falling asleep at nap time or at night
- Waking earlier in the morning
- Waking during the night when this wasn't a problem before.

The Unlikely Problem Of Too Much Napping

By the time your child goes off to kindergarten, he needs to be able to sustain himself an entire day without a nap. Most children get to this point by age four. If your five-year-old still relies on a nap, then you will need to wean him away from this before he starts school.

Start by adjusting his bedtime so he has plenty of time to get in 12 hours of sleep before the family awakes. Adhere to an evening routine that slows activity down and prepares the body for sleep. You don't want him to lie awake, to play or read in bed long after bedtime, or to watch television in bed. Watch his consumption of caffeine and sugary foods from late afternoon on.

Then gradually shorten his naptime in the afternoon from an hour to 45 minutes to half an hour to 20 minutes to zero. This means you'll need to waken him if he sleeps past his allotted time. Do this over a period of several weeks and let your child know what you're doing so he can feel okay about being woken up.

If your five-year-old child truly struggles with no nap, then you may want to put off starting kindergarten for a year. He may be more ready with a bit more time. You also might talk with your pediatrician to make certain there is no underlying condition that causes him to need a nap.

What about an infant or toddler who naps too long? It does seem that if you have someplace to go that's the day your child decides to just sleep and sleep and sleep. Try to be amused by the hand fate has dealt you and either put off your errands or bundle your little sleeper up and go out anyway.

The child who routinely – or at least often – sleeps for hours on end at naptime may not be getting

Dear Rebecca -
Our 11 month daughter is beginning to show some signs of being ready for one long nap. First, her naps have become longer in recent weeks, from 40 minutes each to 90 or 120 minutes each. Most recently her first nap at 9:15 AM has drifted to a later time and she is now resisting that nap.

My question is should we try to avoid the transition to one nap now, before she's even a year old? We like the idea. How can we make this happen?

Dear Dad -
It's not too early to go to one nap if she seems ready.

Often children will show signs of being ready for the transition but can't quite make it to one nap. You can push the first nap later to three or even four hours after getting up for the day and let her nap as long as she wants. You may then need to give her a nap around 3 or 4 pm. This only needs to be long enough to keep her going until bedtime. You will need to wake her from this nap.

Once she gets a little more comfortable staying awake longer in the morning, you can make a nap gradually later and later until it is after lunch enough sleep at night. If she is awake all night and sleeps the day away, then go back to your sleep training techniques. You need to enforce nighttime sleeping so her day-night rhythm is turned back right way round.

An occasional lengthy nap may be triggered by an oncoming illness, by teething, or by an upcoming developmental achievement of some sort. The only worry here is that the nap not run too close to bedtime, so that the nighttime schedule is throw off. Make certain you awaken a napping child in time to have at least 90 minutes to two hours of awake time before bed (longer if the child is older).

It's a bittersweet day when your child gives up his nap. Gone is that lovely break you've enjoyed so long. But the child who no longer needs a nap is growing up. That's a good thing.

Chapter Ten
Waking Up

Sometimes it's not getting your child to sleep that is the problem, it's getting him up. Let's talk about some common waking-up issues that get in the way of a happy start to the day.

Waking Up And Temperament

Just as there are larks and night-owls among adults – people who naturally are early risers or naturally prefer to sleep in – so there are basic differences among children that seem hard-wired into their makeup. Some children find getting out of bed at dawn's early light easy to do. Some children struggle to open their eyes even after the entire family is awake. To a certain extent you can modify these natural tendencies but often what you see is what you get. This is just how your child is.

Blame it on heredity. Probably you or the child's other parent shares the same wake-up pattern. The adults may have learned to adjust their preference to the demands of work or school (if they are naturally late-risers) or to a desire to be coherent after sundown (if they are naturally early-risers). Your child has none of these motivations.

So it works best if you can be accommodating to your child's natural waking-up patterns while you shape them gradually to something that fits the demands of your family's schedule. As we have seen in our discussions of sleeping, circadian rhythms cannot just be turned on and off with a switch but they can be tweaked over time.

Up Too Early

The most commonly-reported waking-up issue is waking up too soon. If you've ever been awakened in the springtime by birds twittering madly when all is still dark, you realize that awake-before-dawn is not so unnatural as it seems. Nonetheless, no one wants to be up at 4:30 or 5:00 am with a child who thinks it's time to get the day started.

Realize, of course, that the baby who still needs to nurse in the night may wake for a feeding at dawn and not be ready to get up at all. This early morning wake-up may be a nuisance for you – by the time you get the child fed and back to bed the sun is up and all chance for more sleep is gone. But this is simply an unfortunate part of the feeding schedule. As the infant gets older and can go longer between feeds, this problem can be managed by tweaking the time of the last feed before you go to bed, so that feeds during the night can be timed to leave you those last precious minutes of the night in peace.

For the slightly older infant or toddler, your best strategy is to treat early morning like the middle of the night. Use one of the back-to-sleep techniques discussed earlier. Make certain there are blackout shades on the windows, especially if it's summertime, to help with the illusion that it's not at all morning.

By the time your child is three or so, you can be more explicit about a wake-up being "too early." Tell the child firmly that it's too early to get up and guide her back to bed. Again room-darkening shades will help here. Make certain, also, that the child is neither too cold nor too warm, since these can make her wake up. The child who is learning to use the potty may wake up in the early morning either because of a wet diaper or because of a desire to use the toilet. Treat this like a middle-of-the-night wake up, doing what's needed to get the child toileted and tucked back in.

Children as young as two can be taught an acceptable wake-up time by setting a nightlight on a timer. The child can only get out of bed (or demand to be got up) if the light is shining. Realize that this light may work like an alarm clock, wakening your child just as a bell would, so set the time to something you really can handle.

Older kids, anywhere from three on up, can be taught to read a digital clock, getting up only when the left-most numeral is a 7 or whatever. This method requires some practice during the day, to avoid misreading of the clock, but it is a handy way to introduce the notion of telling time.

If your child awakens early and knows to stay in his room until an appointed hour, make certain he cannot get into trouble on his own while he's up and you're not. Early morning is prime time for some children to take off all their clothes (including messy diapers), climb out of the crib, climb up on furniture, peer out of windows, fool with outlets and otherwise take advantage of your lack of supervision. The worry of what he's getting into may be enough to make an early riser out of you!

Up Too Early On Weekends

It's a sad truth that children do not understand sleeping-in on weekends. Once you've got your child trained to stay in bed until a decent hour in the mornings, this becomes the default wake-up time for every day, including Saturdays, Sundays and holidays. Part of being a parent includes being up "on time" every day of the week.

As your child gets past the preschool years, you can perhaps trust her to get her own breakfast and keep herself amused until you stumble out to join her. This is what cold cereal and Saturday morning cartoons were made for, after all. But by the time she reaches such a responsible age, you may find that she's involved in soccer practice, dance class, or other good things that will have you not only up but out the door every weekend morning.

Try your best to view getting up on the weekends at the same time as during the workweek as an opportunity instead of a deprivation. You've got more time with your child, after all, and more time for the things you'd like to do together, if you're up and doing early even on your days off.

Crying On Awakening

The loveliest thing is hearing your toddler cooing and talking to himself in his crib as he wakes from his nap or wakes in the mornings. This gives you a few moments to get your own act together before going in to him, smiling and relaxed, to greet him and welcome him back to the day. Nice!

For many parents, though, this is a fantasy. Some children seem to go straight from sleeping to wailing, with no time in between. The day or the afternoon is off to a bad start without even a chance for pleasantries and you've got to drop everything and run to your child to prevent him from going into total meltdown. If this is your child's pattern, how can you fix it?

Try waking him before he wakes. If you know the time he's likely to wake up, go in 10 or 15 minutes early, busy yourself in his room, maybe putting clothes away or straightening up, humming gently and opening the shades. As soon as he stirs, speak softly to him, stroke his tummy, and pour on the charm. See if you can change his pattern from waking-to-cry to waking-to-smile.

Dear Rebecca -
I have a 5 month old who wakes up at the same time every morning. I've tried putting her to bed at different times but she still wakes up at 4:30. She also will rarely take an afternoon nap. I try her normal bed routine but she usually refuses an afternoon nap and by 6 pm she's melting down. Please help!

Dear Mum -
Make sure that she is nice and relaxed, not over tired or under tired when it comes to the afternoon nap. She may only need to be awake for around two hours between naps. Make sure you have a 10 to 15 minute long nap routine, this will help relax her before you try to get her down.

Is she ready to start the day at 4:30 am? Or, are you able to get her back to sleep? If she seems wide awake that early, then take a look at your daily routine. See if she's awake long enough in the evening that she can sleep until a reasonable time in the morning. If she's going to bed at 6 pm, then adjusting her afternoon nap so she can stay up later will help her sleep later in the morning.

Blackout shades can also help, if the problem is worse in the summertime.

Once you've got this going, continue but when you hear him wake be on the other side of the room. Call to him, saying something like, "Hi, there! I'm right here! Did you have a good sleep?" then go to him, pat him, get him up. Eventually, you should be able to be standing outside his room, waiting for him to make a noise so you can call to him and come in. You want to teach your child to let you know he's awake and waiting for you and to realize that he doesn't need to cry to do it.

Fixing this common problem will make for a happier day for both of you.

A Slow, Grumpy Wake-Up

Your older toddler or preschooler – one who is sleeping in a big bed and can get out of her room on her own – may not cry for you to come get her but may wander into the main part of the house, clutching her lovey and with no words for anyone. She may fall asleep again immediately on the couch or may sit and sulk. No, she doesn't want any breakfast. No, she doesn't need to use the bathroom. No, she doesn't want to talk with you. No. No. No.

This is all fine and well if there's no need to be anywhere anytime soon. But if your child is naturally grumpy in the morning and you need her to eat, get dressed, and be out the door to childcare quickly, then her slow start-up can be a problem. The solution

Dear Rebecca -
Our Isabel, 13 months, has been waking screaming from her nap and also at night. She reduced her night sleep from 11 hours with one nap to 9 or 10 hours with two naps. She's only getting an hour and a half of naptime now.

We think she's ready for just one nap, but are wondering if it's screwing with her sleep otherwise. She might be getting molars, her gums are wide. We also just came home from vacation. Where should we start to get things back on track?

Dear Mum -
Give her a few days to settle down from the vacation before trying to change anything with her sleep. The teething is also a big issue. Those molars can be so painful coming through.

Try putting her to bed a little earlier too. I think she's overtired when she goes to bed at night.

is to remember what you can change and be mindful of what you can't. You can't change your child's temperament or her preset body chemistry. She may simply need more time or more support to get her mind and body going in the morning than you do or than her siblings do. You can't change that. What you can change are the schedule and, to a certain extent, her willingness to meet you halfway.

Start by making certain that her bedtime is appropriate and that she has at least 11 hours of sleep before she needs to get up. Make certain that the wake-up time you've set allows enough time for her to get herself ready for the day on a child-size timetable. You may have learned how to get up and be out the door in 30 minutes but your child likely needs much more time. So check both ends of the day: does the wake-up time you've established allow enough time for a child to get ready to leave the house on time and is the bedtime you've set early enough to permit sufficient sleep before that wake-up moment?

Help your child be more efficient in the mornings by doing what you can the night before. If choosing what to eat for breakfast is too hard to do in the morning, help your child make her selection at night. The same goes for choosing what to wear. By helping your child make these decisions when she's thinking clearly, you will relieve her of having to make choices in the morning when she's not up to the task.

Use a timer to help organize the morning schedule. A timer is impersonal and less likely to be resisted. Say,

Dear Rebecca -
Do you have any suggestions on toddler early waking and transitioning to a bed? We are about to transition our 2-year-old climber to a toddler bed due to crib climbing, and are worried about what he'll do when he wakes up at 4 and 5 am.

Currently he gets a sticker reward if he waits to call for us till his toddler clock lights up, and he is able to put himself back to sleep when that happens a lot of the time. I worry that he'll keep himself awake instead when he can roam, and then be tired later.

I would love any tips!

Dear Mum –
I wouldn't be so worried about his being tired during the day as I'd be about what he could get into on his own! So make certain that his room is really as safe as you can make it, even get down to his eye level and see what hazards might be attractive. Make certain that he can't get out of his room and wander the house unsupervised. If his room doesn't have blackout shades, you might want to install some.

Then I'd wait and see. This may be a non-problem, especially since it sounds like he's been able to climb out of his crib on his own already. Good luck!

"I'm setting the timer for three minutes. When the bell rings, it will be time to get dressed." Make certain you have time to help your child if she's not able to get things done herself.

If your child is age three or older, you can talk about the need for her cooperation in the mornings. Do this at a different time during the day, when you both are feeling cheerful and can tackle some problem solving. Explain to her the issue of being grumpy and slow in the mornings and how this makes you both unhappy. Talk about how you can work together to be more efficient. Decide on some things to try the next day (including setting out clothes the night before or making a decision about breakfast before going to bed).

Being able to get up and going in the morning is a key skill but one that needs to be taught. Help your child to master this.

Managing The Switch Of Daylight Savings Time

You may have got your child on a great bedtime schedule and the morning wake-up may be going smoothly. Then the switch to or from daylight savings time happens and everything is off by an hour. How can you get things back on track?

Patience. Within a few days – certainly within a week – you and your child will have adjusted to the new time. Since melatonin is dependent on light levels, and since it's light levels that change relative to the time in daylight savings time, it makes sense that the ability to fall asleep and the tendency to wake are disturbed when we change the clocks. The first few days may be trying but soon things will fall into place.

You might find it helpful to make the switch over a longer period of time than just one day. There's no reason why you can start the time change in your household a week ahead, tweaking the schedule by 10 minutes a day until you're up to a full 60 minutes of difference. If experience has told you that changing the clocks leads to a great deal of upset for your child, or if your child is temperamentally more sensitive to changes than other kids you know, then making the time change gradual may be worth the effort.

Thinking about daylight savings time reminds me of jetlag and all the sleep problems that arise when traveling with children. We'll look at those in Chapter Eleven.

Chapter Eleven
Sleeping Through Life's Disruptions

Everyday life is difficult enough. But every family runs into changes that upset the daily routine and make sleep hard to come by. Many of these changes are good, even wonderful. But because they distract you it's possible you might not even notice their effect on your children until it's obvious that no one is getting any sleep.

Let's walk through some of the most common family disruptions and consider how these might play out at bedtime and what you can do to get things back on track.

Traveling

Imagine travel from the small child's perspective: suddenly the family packs up, gets into the car or on an airplane, straps the child into a car seat for hours on end, and finally winds up in a strange place, with strange beds, strange people, and strange food. Nothing is the same and, from the child's point of view, everything familiar is gone forever. No amount of explanation will clarify things for even a preschool child, who has no sense of geography and no notion of time. No wonder kids get upset and act badly.

Travel is difficult for the adults, too, making them short-tempered and anxious. Children pick up on their parents' emotions – nothing is more essential to their survival than the mental state of Mom and Dad – and they get anxious too. Pretty soon everyone is close to meltdown.

Add in the possibility of jet lag and a child's Difficult or Slow-To-Warm-Up temperament and it's obvious why traveling with small children is not for the faint of heart. Even Easy children will be stretched to the limit by travel.

But visiting relatives or seeing faraway sites is lovely. No need to put these off until your youngest child is six. What's needed to make things go smoothly is plenty of sleep.

As much as possible, stick to your daily routine. Jet lag will get in the way but after a couple days your child will be back on schedule if you *keep* to a schedule. Do not skip naps,especially in the first few days at your destination, make certain your child gets his naps. Adhere to the bedtime routine.

There will probably be issues with getting to sleep and staying asleep. Remember your sleep training techniques and rely on them to get things back to normal. You may need to be content with some level of sleep disruption while you're away from home, but the more you can maintain the usual routine the better.

Realize that when you get home, things will not fall right back into place. If there was jet lag in your vacation spot, there will be jet lag again at home. Your child may be unaccountably clingy, especially if he became used to sleeping as a family all in one room. Again, your sleep training techniques will help you out. Don't delay implementing them, but try to get things back to normal quickly.

Moving To A New Home

Even a move across town to a nicer, bigger place is stressful for adults and children alike. Parents are distracted by all the legal twists and turns, the desire to paint rooms or buy new furniture and perhaps also by whatever inspired the move to begin with, like a new job or new family situation. It's hard to keep the children in mind at such times.

But children are not just baggage, of course, that can be packed up with the good china and unpacked at the new destination. So much changes in a household move and even babies notice. So much that was familiar is replaced by things that are unfamiliar.

There is a temptation to combine a household move with moving a baby out of her parents' bedroom into a room of her own, or moving a toddler out of his crib into a big boy bed. As much as possible, limit the newness. Make these changes one at a time over a period of several months so that there's not too much disruption all at once. Even if it seems like it's time to change your child's sleeping arrangements, put this off until after the move is accomplished and your child seems well-settled.

Dear Rebecca –
My 3 year old daughter has been having trouble getting to sleep ever since she had surgery on her tonsils. She is afraid to be left alone, and her dad or I need to stay in the room with her until she falls asleep. She also claims hunger or thirst at the last minute, and it's hard to tell if she's being truthful or just trying to prolong going to bed. For the first few weeks I understood but now we're ready to get back to where we were before the surgery, if not even a better place - it would be great to just tuck her in and leave the room. We do have a solid bedtime routine which includes reading books together...

Dear Mum -
Try offering a banana before you start the bedtime routine or before brushing teeth. Let her know it's her last chance to eat before the morning. Keep a drink by her bed. Bananas are a great sleep inducing food.

Try gradually moving yourselves towards the door. Sit a little further from her bed every other night until you are out of the room. When reading as part of your routine, make sure that this is in a dim environment. This will help with melatonin production. Melatonin is the sleepy hormone.

Take things nice and slow and I think you'll be back to where you were pre-surgery soon. Good luck!

Depending on your child's age and temperament, a household move can trigger separation anxiety, night terrors, bad dreams, and problems with falling asleep and waking at night. You may find your child wants to sleep in your room or in your bed. Keep in mind that what you permit on the first night in your new home sets what's "normal." Try to adhere to whatever was normal in your old home in making the transition to the new one.

Deal with sleep disruptions with your sleep training techniques and with techniques described earlier for bad dreams and such. Provide your child with the security of a consistent routine. Help him to enjoy the new home without regressing to a more dependent stage.

Adding A New Baby

Regression to an earlier stage is one of the most common reactions of a toddler or preschooler to the arrival of a new baby brother or sister. The infant gets a lot of attention even though he's helpless and incompetent. Certainly the older child might consider mimicking this behavior, by crying, wanting to take back her crib, or wanting to nurse.

But what seems like regression caused by jealousy might simply be regression caused by upset. Even though the birth of a baby is a happy event, parents are tired and distracted. There are odd people in the home – grandparents, friends, maybe a postpartum doula or mother's helper – and many of these people may appear to the older child to get in the way of her access to Mom or Dad and even to the baby. The old familiar routine is turned upside down. Nothing is the way it used to be.

With so much going on, the toddler or preschooler is certain to have trouble taking naps or going to bed at night. The adults might be impatient with such behavior, which will only add to the stress. What's needed is some reassuring normalcy.

When there is a new baby, as much as possible whoever was the one to put the child down for a nap and to bed at night should continue to do this. Sticking to the daily routine and sticking to the naptime and evening routines will help the older child feel secure and that there is some predictability remaining in her life. Instead of delegating the older child's care to a visiting relative, let the relative manage the baby while Mom or Dad settles the sibling.

Toddlers and preschoolers seem able to sleep through just about anything and it is unlikely that midnight care of the new baby will disturb the older child's sleep, even if the baby and the older child sleep in the same room. But the older child may have sleep disruptions of her own, struggling to fall asleep, to stay asleep, and to avoid bad dreams or night terrors. Rely on the sleep training techniques to provide some structure to both the go-to-bed routines and to the way you handle disturbances in the night.

It's easy to think, in your own sleep-deprived state, that the older child should "understand" your need to tend to the new baby and help you out by being "good." This sort of sensitivity is completely beyond the abilities of young children. Despite the difficulties of managing two children's sleep needs, you and your partner (remember to tag team!) will need to be the grownups for both the baby and the older child, even during the night.

Child Illness

Even a minor illness can bother a child's sleep. Whether it's a cold that interferes with a child's breathing, teething that makes his whole head ache, a fever or the flu, being sick is no fun during the daytime and even worse at night. Adding to the problem can be the effects of medications, that might keep a child awake or make him feel strange while it's relieving his symptoms. The experience of the illness can also be upsetting, if it includes vomiting, chills, and the hypersensitivity associated with a fever.

There's not much point in trying to stick with sleep training when a child feels miserable. The best a parent can do is be sympathetic and supportive and help the child rest as best he can. This may mean walking the floor with him, rocking him, or sleeping nearby.

If your child must be hospitalized, the disruption is, naturally, all the greater. Your steady presence is required to help your child stay calm but your own

Dear Rebecca –
Ever since our second child was born 10 weeks ago, our first child has just about quit sleeping. She struggles to fall asleep at night, even though she was doing pretty well before the baby was born, and she wakes a couple times. Combine that with the newborn's waking to nurse and you get a picture of our lives: no sleep. What can we do?

Dear Mum –
You don't say how old your first child is... I'm going to guess that she's under three. And I can't tell if both children are in the same room. If they are, you might find the situation resolves more quickly if you put the baby's bed in a different room (your own, perhaps).

Okay, though, what to do? I suggest you focus on the older child's sleep by using one of the sleep training methods in this book or by going back to whatever method you used before. Since your daughter was doing fine before the baby came, my guess is that you were surprised and unprepared for her sleeplessness and so maybe have thought this would just go away and haven't done much to help her in a deliberate way. By treating this like the problem it is and working on a solution, you might get more sleep quicker.

You should see results in three or four days if you manage to start a plan and are consistent.

Best wishes!

sleep deprivation will begin to take its toll. In a hospital setting, your child's sleep quota is the responsibility of the medical staff, so at least you are relieved of that small worry. But staying healthy and well-rested yourself is a real challenge.

No matter what the malady, child illness disrupts sleep. The time to get things back to a normal routine is after your child is on the mend, as quickly as seems reasonable. Return to your daily routine and to your routines for naptime and evening. Deal with sleep disruptions as you would for any other regression, returning to your sleep training techniques. The quicker you can get your child back to good sleep patterns, the stronger he will become.

A Missing Parent

Many events can remove a parent from home: a business trip, a military deployment, a hospital stay (even for the birth of a baby), and so on. More catastrophic events, like death, incarceration or marital separation, trigger not only the removal of a parent but a cascade of financial and emotional fallout that can complicate things tremendously. Remember that your children will pick up on your psychological state and this will contribute to their anxiety. Anxiety of any sort interferes with sleep.

Even as part of the most benign events, the fact that one parent is missing can cause problems with sleep. It can trigger separation anxiety, clinginess, night terrors, and sleepwalking, as well as garden-variety

Dear Rebecca -
Any advice for dealing with time changes while traveling? We'll have a 3 hour difference to adjust to.

Dear Dad -
You don't have to change schedule at all if you are going away for a week or less. Just keep on the same schedule. If you're going West to East, you'll go to bed later and get up later.

If you are going for longer you don't have to change the full 3 hours, you may just want to change 2 hours.

When making any adjustments with sleep it's always easier going East to West. It's easier to stay up later (going to bed early is tough!). You can go the full two hours right away.

Or, you could go a little slower. Start by working on the waking time. Make it 15 to 30 minutes earlier than your local time. Naps and bedtime will shift the 15 to 30 minutes. Every day or two make another shift with the wake up time, doing the same with the nap time and bedtime.

Keep going until you are on local time.

difficulty in falling asleep and staying asleep. Since the parent won't be able to postpone whatever takes him or her away from home, these reactions on the part of your child simply should be dealt with by redoubling the sleep training or applying more specific methods described in other chapters.

If the family problem is a major one and you are unable to manage your child's sleep problems on your own, do get professional help. Just talking to a knowledgeable person will help you feel more calm and you may get some specific suggestions to help your child.

Be careful to avoid elective absences as much as possible during the 9-to-12-month age, when separation anxiety is at its height and when secure attachment can be at risk. When your child is at this age it's not a good idea, for example to plan a getaway vacation for you and your partner, even if the person who will stay with your child is a much-loved grandparent or nanny. The sleep issues that arise may be very difficult to fix on your return.

Back To Where You Were...

Once you and your child have established a sleep routine, this is your home base. No matter what disruptions come your way, your routine is what you return to, your best method for getting back to peaceful, happy sleep for everyone.

Your calm, matter-of-fact, this-is-the-way-we-do-it attitude will help your child recapture her old patterns of sleeping and waking. This is why teaching your child how to fall asleep was such an excellent idea in the first place.

How To Tell If You Need
A Sleep Consultant

If you think you need help in getting your child to sleep then contacting a sleep consultant is probably exactly what you need to do.

If your child is not sleeping well, you are not sleeping well either. You are not at your best in any aspect of your life and you may be unable to think clearly about your child's sleep issues or find workable solutions. You may have tried one method after another and be frustrated and confused. Your partner may even be blaming you for your child's sleep issues and this makes you feel even worse.

Imagine how relieved you'll feel when you finally get some sleep, when your child finally gets some sleep, and when getting adequate sleep becomes your family's pattern, something you can count on just about every night.

There likely is a sleep consultant somewhere near you. But remember that I am near you, wherever you are. I work with parents by phone and messaging as well as in person. Find out more about my work at www.rebeccamichi.com. Contact me for an initial consultation and to set up a program of coaching and advising.

Getting a good night's sleep is so important, for your child's health and well-being and for your own. If you're struggling with sleep issues, get help now.

You'll feel instantly better about the whole situation and you'll be on the path to solving the issue.

I am a parent, like you. I know what you're going through. I want to help you.

I know how to help you.

If you think you need a sleep consultant, don't delay. Let's get together and solve this problem right now.

For Further Information

American Academy of Pediatrics at www.aap.org

National Sleep Foundation at
www.sleepfoundation.org

Sleep (online journal of research) at
www.journalsleep.org

Sudden Infant Death Syndrome at
www.ncbi.nlm.nih.gov/pubmedhealth/PMH0002533

Temperament and Development (1977). Stella Chess and
Alexander Thomas, Brunner-Routledge.

CPSIA information can be obtained at www.ICGtesting.com
Printed in the USA
LVOW08s0729090913

351533LV00003B/8/P